3—

Barnaby Conrad

"A
Revolting
Transaction"

by Barnaby Conrad

Fiction

THE INNOCENT VILLA

MATADOR

DANGERFIELD

ZORRO: A FOX IN THE CITY

ENDANGERED (with Niels Mortensen)

FIRE BELOW ZERO (with Nico Mastorakis)

KEEPERS OF THE SECRET (with Nico Mastorakis)

Translations

THE WOUNDS OF HUNGER (Spota)

THE SECOND LIFE OF CAPTAIN CONTRERAS (Luca de Tena)

Nonfiction

HOW TO FIGHT A BULL

ENCYCLOPEDIA OF BULLFIGHTING

TAHITI

FAMOUS LAST WORDS

SAN FRANCISCO—PROFILE IN WORDS AND PICTURES

DEATH OF MANOLETE

GATES OF FEAR

MY LIFE AS A MATADOR (Autobiography of Arruza)

LA FIESTA BRAVA

FUN WHILE IT LASTED

"A Revolting Transaction"

by

Barnaby Conrad

ARBOR HOUSE
New York

DEDICATION

To BC III,
with love and appreciation of
his contribution to this book

Acknowledgments

Apart from personal family papers, and the assistance of my cousin, Gloria Christensen, several sources were helpful in reconstructing this famous murder case. An invaluable work was *Death in the Mail*, by Martin Day, published in 1894, from which several quotations appear in the text. Other useful works include *Montana: An Uncommon Land*, by K. Ross Toole and *Pondera*, published by the Pondera History Association, Conrad, Montana. The author also wishes to thank the Denver Public Library for its many kindnesses.

"She was a vile woman and she had vile lovers. Once in the Adirondacks he looked through a crack in the ice-house and saw Mrs. Barnaby and the guide, Mr. Bennett, lying drunk on the floor in the sawdust, and with every indication of a previous revolting transaction having taken place."

—BOSTON GLOBE QUOTING
DR. T. THATCHER GRAVES

"I like poison killings best—
I don't like messy deaths."
—AGATHA CHRISTIE

"It is always a surprise to see that doctors are
such clumsy murderers."
—THOMAS M. McDADE, REFERRING
TO T. THATCHER GRAVES
IN *THE ANNALS OF MURDER*

"Poisoners are generally ineffectual characters,
who feel compelled to lay claim by poison to the rights
which life has denied them."
—JULIAN SYMONS

Prologue

My mother died in 1982 in Santa Barbara, California, at the age of ninety-three. To me fell the task of going through her personal effects and disposing of them.

After three days there remained only one small trunk or large suitcase, with the distinctive LV design of Louis Vuitton. I forced the lock open with a screwdriver and was greeted with a musty smell and several large manila envelopes.

The first contained dozens of letters precious to my mother from her family, such as this one from my father at age sixteen:

> Helena, Montana
> 1903
>
> My Dear Helen:
> Although I know now that I may never be able to call you mine, I shall ever hold you in my heart and if ever I should be tempted to do any unworthy act I would see a vision of your angelic face and be restrained...

And this from my mother's father:

> San Francisco
> 1931
>
> My darling daughter:
> How splendid that you are enjoying Egypt and the wonders of the East and that Barnaby is feeling better! Little

11

Barnaby and Hunt are doing well and look forward to seeing you in a few months...

And one from myself during my bullfighting days:

MADRID
1958

Dear Mother:
I am recovering nicely from that stupid goring and the doctor says that in three weeks...

A packet of Christmas cards and thank-you notes from her seven grandchildren made up the rest of the contents.

The second envelope contained letters from "noteworthy people," such as this one from President William Howard Taft:

WASHINGTON, D.C.
1905

Dear Helen:
Thank you for your lovely note. Mrs. Taft and I enjoyed seeing you at the luncheon and hope to see you next week at...

And from Theodore Roosevelt:

WASHINGTON, D.C.
1915

My dear Little Helen:
I cannot bring myself to address you as Mrs. Conrad, but I send you the heartiest congratulations...

Letters from Alice Longworth Roosevelt to my mother in Puerto Rico, where her father was governor, notes from the popular play-

wright Austin Strong, novelist Stewart Edward White, the explorer
Donald MacMillan and others made up the rest.

The last envelope on the bottom was not really an envelope. It
was a thick brown paper folded into a packet and sealed in three
places with red wax. It was foxed with age and written on the
outside in stilted penmanship were the words:

March 1894
NOT TO BE OPENED BY ANYONE UNTIL 1994!

It was signed by my father's mother, Mabel Barnaby Conrad
Kendall.

I held it in my hand and hesitated only briefly; after all, it was
practically 1994, wasn't it?

I ripped open the paper. Inside, between pieces of cardboard,
were two letters in beautiful handwriting, one short, one long, plus
a covering note in my grandmother's handwriting: "These two letters were obtained from a guard at the prison by my then husband,
John Howard Conrad. They must never be allowed to be seen or
published."

> To Whom It May Concern:
> Upon my solemn Masonic Oath I, T. Thatcher Graves,
> did not have anything to do in any way, shape, manner
> nor deed, with the death of Mrs. Barnaby. I write this
> knowing what the future will soon have in store for me.
>
> To the Coroner: Please do not hold any autopsy upon
> my remains.
>
> The cause of death may be rendered as follows: "Died
> from persecution, worn out, exhausted."
>
> I am respectfully
>
> T. Thatcher Graves, M.D.
> Harvard '71

13

With it was a typewritten manuscript of eight pages entitled, "The True Secret of the Barnaby Murder... One that totally alters the verdict of the famous murder case."

Written in pen across the top of the first page were the words:

> In consideration, for certain sums of money from the Conrad Bank of Montana, I do hereby agree and swear never to try to publish the information contained in this interview with Judge Macon. (signed) Wilson P. Rush.

Attached to the manuscript with a rusty pin was a piece of stationery with the letterhead "Harfield Conrad" addressed to my father:

> August 10, 1909
>
> Dear Cousin Barnaby:
> Thought you'd better know about this—cost our bank quite a penny to suppress it but we couldn't have the slimy creature spreading this bilge about your father. If you hear of the bastard trying to peddle it elsewhere alert us at once.
>
> Best Wishes,
> Har

I began to read with growing amazement and apprehension. Had I just stumbled across proof of a monstrous injustice that had been committed some ninety-one years before? But first, the background.

One

This is the story of my great-grandmother's murder. It was a sensational story in its time, 1891. It was on the front page of American newspapers for more than a year. Two books were written about it, as well as innumerable accounts in magazines, "classic" crime anthologies and legal case histories. This is the first accurate telling of all the elements of the case.

It is still a good story, but not in the way it was then and not for the same reasons. In the first place, it was called, and probably was, the first murder ever committed by mail. (There have been several in the ninety-odd years since.) In the second place, the crime resulted in the longest murder trial in the history of the United States up until that time—almost six weeks. There have been many longer trials since then—the Manson trial, for example, lasted almost half a year. On the other hand, one of the longest murder trials in the history of the Old Bailey in London lasted only seventeen days in 1952—and, coincidentally, that one also concerned a doctor on trial for murdering his elderly, wealthy benefactress.

In the third place the Barnaby murder was considered a very racy murder at the time. Doctors were venerated on a par with ministers. Harvard men were in general highly respected, as were army officers and Masons. A murderer who was first in his class at Harvard Medical School? A Mason and former distinguished army officer under suspicion as a sexual hypnotist, using his powers to seduce, bilk and finally murder a wealthy widow? It was pretty heady stuff.

And there was the wealthy Rhode Island widow, considered eminently respectable, suddenly accused of "revolting transactions" with an Adirondack guide while lying drunk on the sawdust of an icehouse floor. Shocking, especially since it appeared right on the front page of the New York *Times*.

When I came to write it I was tempted to novelize it. But ultimately I felt that tampering with it would ruin it, and that I would forever be saying defensive things like: "But Henry G. Trickey, Jerothmul Bowers Barnaby and Dr. T. Thatcher Graves are not made-up names and they *were* real people, and yes, the whole case did hang on the origin of a single postage stamp and . . ."

So I have written it as factually as possible, starting at the beginning. I first heard about the case when I was very young.

Something had troubled me that afternoon at school and I was having a hard time keeping it to myself as I fidgeted on my grand-mother's Mediterranean-style veranda.

I was eight and spending the year with the sixty-nine-year-old lady at her Santa Barbara estate while my parents traveled abroad. The year was 1930 but the Great Depression hadn't made a dent in her style of living. The butler wheeled the tea service out on the red-tiled veranda and the maid passed rectangles of cinnamon toast. Below us sloped the long lawn, and the little gravestone over my father's beloved dog "Pucky" glistened in the fading sunlight. Tailored rose gardens overlooked placid Montecito and the channel with the distant islands afloat in it like purple battleships. I squirmed in the wicker chair, longing to blurt out the tale I had heard from an older boy at school.

"One or two, dear?" asked my grandmother in her gentle and rarefied accent which always sounded slightly British to me. The silver teapot on its gimbal simmered over the Sterno flame. She tilted it forward over the Meissen cup.

"Three," I said.

She clucked disapprovingly as she picked up the sugar cubes

with the silver tongs and plopped them into the imported Oolong. I studied her with an interest I had never had before. She was a chic, composed old lady dressed in a red velvet hostess gown, a pearl "choker," and a lot of diamonds—*big* diamonds. Was it possible that she could ever have been involved in such a thing, a thing that other children were now teasing me about? Her name originally was Mabel Barnaby and she had been born in Providence, Rhode Island. A cousin had said recently: "She pronounced it Mah-*bell* after only one week of living in Paris—and *she* from Providence!" She was first married to my father's father, John Howard Conrad. After ten stormy years of marriage and three children, they were divorced, and she was now married to a bearded gentleman named George Choate Kendall, whom my brother and I were required to call "Pater" (and who looked and sounded like the ubiquitous Commander Whitehead of past times). As we drank our tea, Pater stretched out on the wicker chaise longue and studied the Wall Street *Journal*, a task that seemed to occupy most of his day. He stroked his yellow-white mustache with one finger, sighed, and periodically made a sound like "ee-yah" to himself. He would cup his hand on his forehead and then drag it slowly down his face; at the end of the trip his eyes, which had been open, would then be closed. The process always reminded me of flicking one's finger down venetian blinds.

Suddenly I could contain it no longer. I turned to my grandmother.

"Your mother was murdered!" I accused, as only an eight-year-old can accuse.

The old lady turned slowly and glared at me glacially through her lorgnette. Then she snapped it shut.

"Where on *earth* did you hear such a story, child?" She made it a statement rather than a question and her veiled anger scared me.

"John...at school," I mumbled, beginning to regret having brought it up. "His mother—well, she—said she'd read in the newspaper—the Sunday supplement—where. . . ."

"Not accurate," said Mabel Barnaby Conrad Kendall. She stood up and banged the cup and saucer onto the tray with finality. "Tell him it's not accurate."

She gathered up the train of her red velvet gown and swept from the veranda.

"Not at all," echoed Pater absently as he continued to read. "Eee—yah—not accurate at all, dear boy."

Years later, I asked my father about the matter. His answer seemed purposefully vague; he was the most honest of men, but I knew he was not being honest about this. He said uncomfortably: "I was a mere child when it happened." Then he added: "I think maybe her doctor did it to get her money." I don't believe he knew any more than that about the case which was, in its time, as famous as the Lizzie Borden murders or the Hall-Mills murder. Then he added gratuitously, "I never liked my father."

I did not think about the case again for many years. Then, in 1962, I read in True magazine an abbreviated account of my special murder, written by Lewis Thompson and Charles Boswell. There I finally learned some of the highlights of the mysterious skeleton in our family closet:

In 1891 my great-grandmother, Mrs. Jerothmul Bowers Barnaby, a wealthy widow, left her Victorian mansion on Broadway in Providence, Rhode Island, and traveled to the West with her friend, Mrs. Edward Worrell, Sr. In Denver she was poisoned at the home of Mrs. Worrell's son. The poison had arrived by mail addressed to her as a gift.

Suspicion immediately fell on six people, among them Mrs. Worrell. Even her own daughter, my grandmother, was viewed with suspicion, and there were more prime suspects to come. Investigation narrowed the list to one suspect, who was soon indicted. The bizarre crime, the investigation, the manner of the indictment of the suspect, and the trial were unique in the annals of American criminology. It was the first time that the mails had been used for murder, which raised the legal question of where the murder was supposed to have been committed, and hence where the trial should be held. The package was mailed by the murderer in Boston, but the victim died in Denver.

"The bullet was fired in one state," said a law expert rhetorically, "but the victim fell dead in another state two thousand miles away. Where did this crime occur?"

The trial was ultimately held in Denver.

Though brief, the Thompson-Boswell account I read of the Barnaby murder was absorbing, and it never left my mind. I always wondered how accurate the account was. I decided to undertake my own research about the murder.

I told my brother about it and he said, "And did they convict the right person?"

"No doubt about it," I said, "guilty as hell."

Within two weeks doubts began to set in, almost from the moment my research began (and before I came across the letters in my mother's trunk). By a splendid coincidence, a few days later I received a letter from an unknown cousin, a Mrs. Gloria Christensen of Providence, Rhode Island.

"We've never met," the letter began, "but my mother was a Barnaby, her father being Abner Barnaby, Jerothmul's brother. Therefore you and I are cousins, and so I just thought I'd write and say hello. I have always been interested in genealogy and for twelve years was in the office which approved of all applicants for the National Mayflower Society. (Did you know that you are descended from Richard Warren who was a passenger on the *Mayflower*?)"

She went on to say she had read some of my books and asked if I had ever heard of an extremely rare book called *Death in the Mail*. It was written by Martin Day, a newspaperman who had covered the Barnaby murder case. She had inherited one of the very few existing copies, and by any chance would I like a Xeroxed copy?

19

I had expected a pamphlet, a cursory resume of what facts I already knew about the case. What arrived a week later was a volume of 450 pages with thirty illustrations. Written less than a year after the trial, the first page started with a flood of Victorian verbiage in the journalistic manner of the time; the florid language was amusing, almost a satire:

> The seventeenth century records many instances of beautiful but intriguing women contracting unsuitable marriages, where the flowers of May were mingled with the withered leaves of January, and an expectant estate filled the cup of poison that dissolved the marriage tie and sent one partner into eternity and enabled and permitted the other to revel in vice and luxury for a few short years. . . .
>
> The era was passed when poison was imparted by the lips, by the pressure of the hand, by the pommel of a saddle, by the fragrance of the rose or the perfume of the bottle. . . .
>
> The crime which this volume discloses is one of subtlety and craft and covers three great States of the Republic—Rhode Island, where it was conceived; Massachusetts, from which it was dispatched; and Colorado, where it was consummated. For the first time in the history of this or any other country wherein the mail seems to be, and is, a member of the universal family which participates in the blessings of diffused intelligence, it has become a partner in the commission of the second crime—treason being the first—in the annals of the human world. . . .
>
> Seldom have the merry nuptial bells bent their melodious and blithesome music to the solemnization of the union of a happier and more responsive couple than Jerothmul Bowers Barnaby and Josephine A. Reynolds

in the city of Providence, Rhode Island, in the fall of
1857....

Once the initial pyrotechnics were over the author got down to
basics and some good solid reporting. Part of the case's appeal had
been that nearly all the principals were prominent and seemingly
staid and respectable, but as I leafed through the pages some of
the paragraphs about my proper great-grandmother fairly leaped
out at me. For example, I was dismayed to read the testimony of
a newspaper reporter with the Dickensian name of Henry Trickey.
He reported that Mrs. Barnaby's doctor, T. Thatcher Graves, had
stated after the woman's death and even before her funeral: "She
was a vile woman and had vile lovers and once in the Adirondacks
he had looked through a crack in the icehouse and saw Mrs. Barnaby and the guide, Mr. Bennett, lying drunk on the floor in the
sawdust, and with every indication of a *revolting transaction* having
taken place."

Another paragraph began: "The doctor informed Mrs. Barnaby
that while her late husband, Jerothmul, had left her only $2,500
a year income, he had almost casually given a present of $100,000
to Mrs. Phettiplace, *his mistress*, shortly before he died."

And there were more surprises in the book. For example, on
one of the half-blank pages some previous reader had pasted a
faded newspaper clipping from the Providence *Journal* dated 1893,
a year after the trial, and bearing supplementary information which
the Xerox machine had impartially reproduced along with the book's
page:

HELENA, MONTANA—Sept. 26—Social circles here
were given a shock this morning by the announcement
that John Howard Conrad, a leading citizen and ac-
counted extremely wealthy, has sued his wife, Mabel
Barnaby Conrad, for divorce asking for custody of three
minor children [one of whom was my father]. He charges

his wife with intimate and improper conduct with several prominent Montanans, including his business partner and brother-in-law. Mrs. Conrad's mother was the victim in the sensational and mysterious Barnaby murder case which was tried in Denver last year. Mr. Conrad spent $38,000 [also reported as $78,000] of his own money to bring the murderer to justice.

Last night, it is a current report on the streets, there was a big row at the house in which Conrad, his wife, the coachman and Chinese cook participated, the coachman using a stick and the Chinaman a skillet. Conrad came out of the melee in bad condition and left the house for a lawyer's office where the complaint was made out and filed today.

First my Victorian great-grandmother, next my staid great-grandfather, then my proper grandmother! I had not met my great-grandparents, of course, but could that ultra-stuffy granny that I had known so well really be the same person in the clipping? I could not imagine it possible. And not one, not two, but several "revolting transactions!" (A ludicrous and almost sacrilegious image came into my mind as I read this—I could not envision Granny putting down her ever-present lorgnette even during the transacting.)

I was intrigued now and began to research the entire case thoroughly. The noted San Francisco lawyer, Melvin Belli, loaned me an impressive tome, *American State Trials*, volume 13, wherein the trial is dealt with thoroughly and enjoys a place of honor next to the Dred Scott case. But it was too legally dry and lacked the information that I wanted. I went to Denver to try to recapture the excitement of so many years ago. The newspapers filed away in the public library and in the Colorado Historical Society were invaluable in giving a picture of the furor that the Barnaby affair had stirred up; have many murder cases at any period and in any country monopolized the front pages of a big city's newspapers for almost ninety days? With growing amazement I spent many hours spelunking in the cavernous stacks of the library with a microfilm projector.

After a few days I felt a need for some evidence beyond reading matter to give me a feel of the concrete actuality of the legendary crime. For example, what had happened to the odd-shaped bottle of poisoned liquid which had started it all? I wanted to hold it in my hands, read the ironic message pasted on it, smell the remaining contents. I went to the basement of the City and County Records, Criminal Division, where such things are kept. The officials were very cooperative and of course knew the case, but "Oh dear, all that sort of thing going back to before 1910 was thrown out some years ago when we moved into this new building." Optimistically I kept thinking I would turn up someone who had firsthand knowledge of the case and some special evidence and heretofore unknown facts. I had to remind myself that even ten-year-old John Schermerhorn, who dramatically produced the missing and all-important postage stamps, would now be over a hundred years old.

I decided to visit the office building of Edward Worrell, Jr., the son of Mrs. Barnaby's traveling companion, where the fatal bottle had been received by my great-grandmother. I took a taxi to the corner of Arapahoe and Fifteenth Streets in the heart of downtown Denver and looked for the building. I was disappointed to see that it had been razed and replaced by a parking lot.

I then set out to find the house where the victim had drunk the poison and died. Of course, I prepared myself, it was highly unlikely that a wooden house of that vintage would have survived Denver's building progress, but at least I wanted to see the location.

The esteemed author and poet, Thomas Hornsby Ferrill, offered to drive me out to look for it. Not far from the center of the city we came to rows of what once must have been fashionable homes on the outskirts of town. Now they are generally run-down and

23

badly in need of paint. Ferrill kept up a running historical commentary as I looked for 2226 Williams Street.

"There's where Buffalo Bill died, and Jack Dempsey was born, and Doug Fairbanks lived over there, and here's where Kit Carson—"

We came to the address. In spite of some structural changes, I knew instantly from drawings in the old newspapers and books that it was the original house. Two stories with a porch, it was painted a bright yellow and well kept. I rang and a handsome black woman came to the door.

"Do you mind if I take a photograph?" I asked. "My great-grandmother once stayed in this house."

"You mean—the lady who was murdered?" Mrs. Daniel Page asked calmly. "Won't you come in?"

She explained that they had owned the house for twenty-five years, and except for the wallpaper her family had kept the woodwork and everything about the same as it must have been almost one hundred years ago.

At last I stood in the very room where Mrs. Barnaby had died. I suddenly got a tingling feeling of the reality of the persons and events that were involved in this historic affair. For the first time it all came to life and ceased merely to be a "case."

As we drove away from the house, Ferrill added to that feeling when he said: "By glory, how spooky! I knew I'd been in that house before! Now I remember—I used to take out a girl who lived there when we were kids."

"What was her name?" I asked casually.

"Worrell," said Ferrill. "Phyllis Worrell—great girl. Took a picture of her on graduation day that I'll show you."

I had met someone of flesh and blood who had touched this fictionlike tale, however remotely.

For the next year I continued my research. This family skeleton of mine was no ordinary affair; it was a complex matter, featuring a large cast of characters, and it involved my going to such diverse

24

places as Chester, Pennsylvania, Helena, Boston, Providence, San Francisco and the Adirondacks. My mother's memory of some of the protagonists was a help, and I also had the constant, invaluable and imaginative research of my newfound cousin, Gloria Christensen. One of the accounts of the case she sent me reported District Attorney Stevens' opening address at the trial, which began:

> The crime which is the subject of inquiry at this trial has no precedent or parallel in the history of the world. It is unique, original, cowardly, dastardly and infamous. . . .

The year was 1891. Jack the Ripper had done his dirty work three years before. Lizzie Borden was a year and five months away from performing her unfilial acts. But why even mention those messy sordid happenings? The Barnaby murder was such a genteel, tidy and well-bred affair.

It all started on a fine spring day in Denver with a pleasant jaunt to the country. . . .

Two

The day she was murdered, Monday, April 13, 1891, was a pleasant one, and Mrs. Josephine Barnaby enjoyed it thoroughly. Accompanied by her traveling companion, Mrs. Edward Worrell of Chester, Pennsylvania, she spent the day at a ranch in the countryside near Denver and returned by train and an elegant open carriage pulled by a matched team of grays.

Although she had visited the city before, Mrs. Barnaby repeatedly expressed her delight in the crystalline air and the glistening grandeur of the snow-covered Rockies, and she sounded for all the world like the freshest of tourists. After a fiery sunset the evening chill set in quickly and the driver sped the carriage toward 2226 Williams Street, where the two women were staying with Mrs. Worrell's son and daughter-in-law. When Mrs. Barnaby began to complain of the cold, Mrs. Worrell cheered her by suggesting, "A little hot toddy will fix you up just fine, Josephine."

Mrs. Worrell, though younger than Mrs. Barnaby, appeared to be the elder because of her straight, thin-lipped mouth, severe eyebrows and sharp features. A casual observer would not have guessed from their polite conversation and friendly manner that they had quarreled violently only a week earlier.

"Oh, won't it just!" Mrs. Barnaby agreed eagerly. "Let's try the present from my unknown admirer, shall we?"

. She was referring to the strange-looking bottle which had been delivered several days earlier, before her arrival in Denver. Addressed to her, it bore a Boston postmark and the cryptic label:

"Wish you a Happy New Year. Please accept this fine old Whiskey from your friend in the woods."

"Probably from Ed Bennett," Mrs. Barnaby had remarked, pleased at the thought, "that handsome guide in the Adirondacks, the one I've told you about. But why 'Happy New Year' in April?"

Once a stunning blond, the wealthy widow Barnaby, now a youthful-looking fifty-five, wore her iron-gray hair short and carefully coiffured. She was a little plump and no longer stunning, but her face was pleasantly pink and she had a good laugh, and the little veins in her cheeks like the threads in a dollar bill revealed her fondness for her evening toddy. Since the birth of one child, she had suffered from a partial paralysis of one arm and occasionally a slight stammer and groping for a word.

In spite of the pampered and privileged life she had always lived, she was not well read, educated, witty or very intelligent. For example, today on the train she had tried to get into the book Dr. Graves had sent her, Kipling's newly published *The Light That Failed*, but she soon put it down in favor of the latest issue of the Ladies Home Journal with its sentimental serial by Sarah Orne Jewett. Even this she did not finish, preferring to stare out at the scenery.

With all her shortcomings, however, Josephine Barnaby did have a certain zest and a childlike appeal that had attracted more people's friendship than one would have thought. She was "a good sport," trusting, vivacious, laughed easily, and repeatedly said that she "took life as it came." She liked "a good naughty story," a couple of drinks, the company of an attractive man, and travel—"as long as I don't have to go to too many cathedrals and museums."

Her husband, Jerothmul Bowers Barnaby, called J.B., whom she had married when she was twenty-one, had been dead two years. In addition to the mansion—called the "Castle" by the citizens of Providence—he had left an estate of $1,700,000 (comparable today to about twelve million, tax free). She didn't miss the overpowering, overbearing J.B. much. He'd always been so busy

28

with his famous prize-winning harness horses or running for governor or traveling for some business or political reason. And with his mistress.

In the beginning she had tried to help him, to be a good wife and "silent partner" in his endeavors, but he had not felt the need of any such help. He liked to bellow a quote from his favorite writer, Mark Twain: "All you need in this life is ignorance and confidence and success is sure!"

He had started with a men's clothing store and then added more branches around New England and the Midwest until he had a chain of eight; in those days it was a new concept of business, and it proved to be highly profitable.

His enterprises brought in money faster than he could spend it, no matter how hard he tried. He loved to "throw a shindig," and he once gave a ball for two thousand people in his "castle" on Broadway that was said to be the grandest ever given in the state of Rhode Island. Especially for the occasion he redid the gardens and added a lavish billiards room, complete with viewing boxes and bleachers around the tables where spectators could sit in comfort, sip champagne and watch the games.

"I admire to live well," was one of his most frequent boasts. The wedding he gave his eldest daughter Mabel when she married John Howard Conrad from Montana was legendary. In addition, he presented his new son-in-law with an entire office building up the street from the Barnaby store, which he christened the Conrad Building, and which still stands at Westminster and Aborn Streets.

But Josephine saw, to her sadness, that in spite of his efforts, money, banquets, servants, decorations and orchestras, many of the politically and socially important Eastern families he had hoped to lure to his home never came; his money was too new and he was a social climber and politician, people said.

And Josephine knew what others knew, that he had a reputation for "having women," which didn't help his social or domestic situation. He was an eccentric who enjoyed his money too much for a New Englander. (In 1943 an elderly Providence cab driver told my brother: "I remember how your great-grandfather used to drive down Broadway from his house to his store with those prize trotters of his. He had a stopwatch and he'd leave the mansion exactly at 8:05 every day, trying to beat his record. Along the way, mothers, knowing exactly the prescribed time he'd be tearing by their houses, shooed their children off the street before those two big bays came booming down the boulevard!")

His personality cowed and overwhelmed Josephine. One simply never knew what the man would do next.

He used to throw free clothing from the roof of his store at Westminster and Dorrance to the scrambling crowds below. Once he took one of his fifteen fine harness horses, put it in the show window of his store, and gave it away to the person who came closest to guessing its weight. People talked about him behind his back but they increasingly patronized his stores.

In 1885 he ordered a fantastic tomb to be built at Swan Point Cemetery for $50,000. When entering the cemetery the monolith is the first thing one sees. Standing fifty-five feet high, it is made of Vermont granite and Italian marble with weeping angels at the base and a Romanesque figure at the top. He declared that it was created in memory of one of their three daughters, Harriet, who had died in her teens, but everyone knew it was a monument to old J.B. himself, to be ready when he died.

Which, incredibly and suddenly, he did in 1889 at the age of fifty-nine, slumping over in his carriage just as he was about to slap the reins down on his team for his ritual morning tear down Broadway. As soon as he was installed in the vault, Josephine Barnaby began to live for the first time in years. She traveled to the Adirondacks with her handsome doctor, T. Thatcher Graves, and she went west and south. On this western trip she had been to Pasadena, Arrowhead, Del Monte and Santa Barbara, where she had taken the baths for her bad arm, and then on to San Francisco and now Denver, a city she enjoyed. Her friend Mrs.

Worrell had been delighted to accompany her from her home in Chester, Pennsylvania, because it would allow her to visit her newly married son, Edward, Jr. And because Denver was such fun. And because Mrs. Barnaby was paying for every cent of the trip.

Now the two women in the carriage rolled swiftly past the magnificent houses of the Denver elite—the Sacred Thirty-six as they were known, the bonanza-rich, inner society born of the fabulously rich silver strikes of the late 1870s and 1880s. At 1340 Pennsylvania Street they passed the granite-trimmed brownstone mansion fronted by ornate lions that was soon to become the home of the Unsinkable Molly Brown. On Capitol Hill Mrs. Worrell pointed out the huge Horace Tabor house where five gardeners, two coachmen and two footmen were employed just to do the outside work for the old senator and his glamorous Baby Doe. Tabor had left his prim wife for the beautiful blond whose affairs and scandalous marriage would ultimately be the core of books, films and an opera; they had recently had a baby, named (by William Jennings Bryant) Rose Mary Echo Honeymoon Silver Dollar Tabor, known simply as Silver.

At that time Tabor was making as much as $80,000 a month from his various mines, and after performances in the Tabor opera house—one of the grandest in the world—the senator and the notorious Baby Doe would frequently give lavish champagne suppers to such international luminaries as Lily Langtry, Lillian Russell, Sarah Bernhardt and Otis Skinner.

Denver, a bustling new city of 157,000, was an exciting place in a fascinating era. It was a lavish, civilized and opulent time in American history. There was some trouble, even famine among the farmers of the Midwest, mine strikes in Montana and labor troubles in New York and rumors of problems in South America. But for the most part in 1891 there was a feeling of calm, twenty-six years after the Civil War.

31

Denver, still fighting its image of "the wild and uncouth West," prided itself on keeping up with the fashions, styles and luxuries as well as any other city in America. It had splendid restaurants, two world-famous hotels, the Windsor and the Brown Palace, and— very shortly—it was to have something it had never had before— a sensational murder and a trial that would attract the attention of the nation.

Three

The street light had just been turned on when the carriage drew up in front of Edward Worrell, Jr.'s house on Williams Street. The driver helped the two women out and escorted them to the door. The two-story house, while not lavish, was a charming one in a new suburb on the edge of town. Denver's "nicest" wealthy young couples lived in this district; twenty-nine-year-old Ed Worrell, an aggressive up-and-coming stockbroker in the firm of Schermerhorn and Worrell, and married recently to a Denver girl from a prominent family, would not have lived anywhere else.

As they went up the stairs, Mrs. Barnaby said, "I don't know about you, Florence, but I'm almost dead! Had a wonderful time, but I'm cold and exhausted. Will you join me with a little whiskey?"

"Certainly," said Mrs. Worrell. "Shall I call Nellie?"

"Don't bother, Flo—I'll do it."

"Just a small one, Josephine—remember, we're a mile above sea level."

There on the mantel over the fireplace was the strange-looking bottle. Mrs. Barnaby picked it up, reread the pasted-on Happy New Year message and smiled. It wasn't even a proper whiskey bottle; the raised letters on the glass proclaimed Leibig's Extract of Meat.

"That Ed Bennett!" she said with a laugh. "My, he's such a scamp."

"You do like him a lot, don't you, Josephine?"

"But he's very much married, damn it all!"

33

Mrs. Worrell smiled and said as she left, "Since when has that bothered you, Jo?"

Mrs. Barnaby put a cylinder on the Ediphone, turned the machine on, and to the tune of "The Blue Danube" did a little waltz into the kitchen, holding the bottle like a dancing partner. The young Swedish girl said good evening and asked if she could help. Nellie got two toddy glasses for Mrs. Barnaby, put some hot water from the kettle in them, and then Mrs. Barnaby filled them with the brown liquid from the bottle. She carried them upstairs and took them into Mrs. Worrell's bedroom. She handed one to Mrs. Worrell, sat on the bed, raised her glass and said cheerfully: "Happy days. Here's to that naughty boy in the woods."

What happened next was testified—and sworn to—by Mrs. Worrell some time after the events:

> I drank down my glassful and as soon as I'd swallowed it I exclaimed "the vile stuff." I repeated that three or four times. Mrs. Barnaby never said a word. She just sat there sipping the liquor. In a little while she said, "I must say, it's *not* very good." Inside of five minutes the puckering taste in my mouth that instantly followed drinking abated, and intense internal burning commenced. Inside of ten minutes I was in great pain and rapidly getting sick to my stomach. Twenty minutes after I drank the stuff I was like a mad woman. The family could do nothing with me. I felt that I'd been poisoned, but they laughed at that, saying, "Mrs. Barnaby drank it and she's all right. You were probably very tired and the liquor overcame you." I knew better, and in a frenzy I waited for death. Then Mrs. Barnaby began to be sick too. Her symptoms were so similar to mine the household got frightened and several doctors were called. Until two o'clock in the morning I was in the greatest agony, and then the nausea gradually disappeared. My stomach

Mrs. Josephine Barnaby
The victim

Jerothmul Bowers Barnaby
Her late, wealthy husband

was in a terrible condition, however. Mrs. Barnaby grew steadily worse throughout the night. The next day, Tuesday, as I lay in bed wondering about the terrible event of the past night, I felt the presence of somebody in the doorway, and looked up to see Mrs. Barnaby. She looked terrible, a specter. "Go to bed," I exclaimed, "moving around like that will kill you!" On Wednesday, despite her nurses' orders, she came in again, and this time I saw it was useless to protest. "Sick—very sick," she gasped, "but I'm going to fight this off, and you can bet your life I'll hunt down whoever did this wicked thing. I swear," she whispered. "I don't think Ed Bennett sent it—he just couldn't have done such a thing, could he? I mean, even if he is mentioned in my will for so much money? Maybe Sallie Hanley—my secretary—she hated me, she threatened me. If it really contains poison I know what I'll do—first get a chemical analysis made, and then just go ahead with whatever has to be done. Dr. Graves will know what to do."

She mentioned "Doctor Graves" twice more and Mrs. Worrell asked Mrs. Barnaby if she should wire Graves, her personal physician, who was back in Providence.

"Why trouble him?" murmured Mrs. Barnaby. "It's such a long way. But, oh, if Tom Graves were here he could make me well! Tom can do anything!"

She grew worse, and Edward Worrell urged her to send for Dr. Graves. Finally on Saturday Worrell sent a wire to him:

MRS. BARNABY DANGEROUSLY ILL. COME IF YOU WISH TO SEE HER ALIVE.

The same wire was sent to her daughter, Mrs. John Howard Conrad, in Helena, Montana. The other daughter, Maud, twenty-one and unmarried, was traveling somewhere in Europe. Mrs. Barnaby, in fact, was estranged from both her daughters and had been since the death of her husband and the resultant litigation over the will.

On Sunday, April 19, Mrs. Barnaby's condition worsened. The doctors stood helplessly by as she sank.

"Who could have done this to me?" she moaned once. "Who?"

Mrs. Worrell was in Mrs. Barnaby's room at the end, which came at two P.M. "She didn't say anything at the last moment," Mrs. Worrell recalled, "she just turned her face to the mountains and smiled sweetly, and—and—died."

Ed Worrell called Rogers, the leading undertaker, and instructed him to "keep the body a while—there may be an investigation."

A telegram informing Dr. Graves of her death was sent Sunday night. But he did not receive it until after sending this one addressed to Mrs. Barnaby:

KEEP UP GOOD COURAGE. I LEAVE AT ONCE TO COME TO
YOU. WAS IN MASSACHUSETTS WHEN TELEGRAM ARRIVED.

But he did not appear in Denver. Another telegram was sent to his wife asking for the doctor's whereabouts. A telegram arrived on Wednesday from Mrs. Graves.

PROBABLY MISSED CONNECTION IN CHICAGO. HOLD RE-
MAINS TILL MY HUSBAND ARRIVES. KITTY GRAVES

Why, one naturally asks, was it so important to have Dr. Graves— or any doctor—come all the way to Denver from the East? Especially once the woman was dead? And she *was* dead. Like Dickens' Marley, there was absolutely no doubt about her demise.

The answer is that T. Thatcher Graves was more than Mrs. Barnaby's physician. How much more is open to conjecture. There is no doubt that he was her business agent and had her power of attorney and that since the death of her husband Mrs. Barnaby had depended greatly upon him. In fact, she was almost unable to function without his advice and treatments. On this western trip she had written for, and received, three separate shipments of medicine for nervousness as well as general health tonics.

Although he had left the East Sunday night and was expected to arrive in Denver on Wednesday evening at six-fifteen, Dr. Graves, inexplicably, did not show up as scheduled. He did not step off the train until Friday morning, five days after Mrs. Barnaby's death. He immediately hired a carriage and told the driver to go to the Worrells' house.

Tall, well dressed and startlingly handsome with full sideburns and moustache, the doctor at fifty years of age exuded an air of quiet calm, competence and self-confidence. The next day the Denver newspaper was to describe him this way.

> His appearance is very distinguished. Of fine phy-
> sique, ... he is the object of general observation. He is
> keen and entertaining in conversation with a pair of blue
> eyes that are wonderfully penetrating and in keeping
> with his genial manner and cheery voice. His gray hair
> curls becomingly and his step is light and prompt. He
> is a man who once seen would be remembered.

Indeed, Thomas Thatcher Graves was a man of astonishing attributes, intellect and diligence, and had been a success in a number of diverse fields. Born in Norwich, Connecticut, in 1841, the son of a distinguished lawyer, he was educated at the academy at East Thompson and did outstanding work in science and English. He went into the Civil War at the first opportunity as a young man. He was made a Union officer, quickly attaining the rank of major in spite of his youth. When Richmond fell he was, at the age of twenty-four, aide-de-camp to General Wertsell, whose forces

37

occupied the city on April 3, 1865. The next day Lincoln entered the fallen Confederate capital and Graves was chosen to escort the President. Together they visited the prison and the evacuated home of Jefferson Davis—the White House of the Confederacy (now the Confederate Museum). Lincoln amused himself by sitting in Davis' chair, clutching his lapels, and giving a flowery imitation of Davis' speeches. Later, on a mission for General Wertsell, Graves called on the family of Robert E. Lee.

After the war Graves attended Harvard and was graduated first in his class from the medical school in 1871. Subsequently he traveled and practiced in Zanzibar and Florida. Later he lived in Connecticut, and shortly before Mr. Barnaby's death he moved with his beautiful young wife, Kitty, to a house in Providence which was across the street from the Barnaby mansion. Specializing in nerve diseases he soon built up a good practice in Providence; among his patients was Mrs. Barnaby. He was prominently identified with the Grand Army of the Republic and was at one time elected to the office of Medical Director of the Rhode Island department. He was a dedicated member of the Union Congregational Church in Providence and he frequently gave talks on the war, travel and religion. He also did research work on medicines and some of his patented products—advertised in newspapers and magazines—sold well. However, he would take all of the profits and put them back into his latest experiments.

"I chided him once about that," said a Providence banker, "and he simply said, 'Bill, do you realize the benefits to mankind if I could come up with a reliable medicine that would foretell fits and strokes?'"

Yes, as the Denver newspaper said, Graves was a man to remember. And that was written even before the trial had begun. Little did Graves know, as the carriage horse clopped along these tranquil tree-lined streets with the smell of spring in the air, that at that moment a telegram was being sent from Montana that would dramatically change the course of his life. It was being sent to the

38

head of the Pinkerton Agency in Colorado by my grandfather, John Howard Conrad, a blunt, wealthy, ruthless man with tremendous drive and many of the less attractive attributes of a bulldog.

Unsuspecting, Dr. Graves alighted from the carriage at 2226 Williams Street, paid the cabby, and walked up the brick steps to the porch of the house. He rang the doorbell and in a moment a pretty blond girl opened it.

"Good evening," said T. Thatcher Graves, bowing slightly. "I believe I am expected."

a Happy New Year
ept this frns old
from your friend
woods.

The poisoned bottle

Wish you a Happy New Year
Please accept this fine old
Whiskey from your friend
in the woods

The message on the bottle

Four

Nellie Nelson, the sixteen-year-old Swedish maid, opened the front door that morning. Her eyes widened at the sight of the well-dressed and handsome man who had rung the doorbell.

"You must be the doctor," she said in her strong accent as she took his hat and coat with the velvet collar.

Laura Worrell came out of the parlor, a pale brown-haired woman of twenty-three with glasses and a pronounced lisp.

"Doctor Graves—we're so glad you're here!" She led him into the living room where her husband and mother-in-law waited. Ed Worrell, skimming a newspaper nervously, was sitting in an anti-macassared chair by the bay window puffing a cigar. His mother lay on the red plush chaise longue, her legs covered by a Shetland robe. Laura Worrell's grandmother, Mrs. Nancy Allen, sat hunched and hollow-eyed rocking steadily in her chair in a corner and working on a piece of crewel stretched on a round hoop. Worrell jumped up and went to the doctor.

"By God, Graves," he said, "you've finally got here." A muscular young man, he had the same disapproving mouth and frown as his mother. "Thank God and welcome!"

"You must be Ed," said Dr. Graves, shaking his hand. He bowed to the old lady in the corner. Then he turned to the woman on the chaise longue. "And you are Florence Worrell?"

"I am," said Mrs. Worrell in her stern and abrupt fashion, holding out her hand to him. "Excuse my not rising. I am not totally well yet."

"We have lost a friend, you and I," said Graves sadly, taking

41

her hand in both of his. "A great friend, one of the best friends I ever had. When did she first suffer the stroke?"

"Stroke?" said Mrs. Worrell.

"I assumed it was a stroke. Or was it an attack?" said Graves. "But she had a reasonably good heart."

"Dr. Graves—" said Worrell.

"Not what you'd call a strong heart, but—"

"We expected you Wednesday night," said Worrell, stabbing out his cigar in an ashtray, "and here it is Friday. We needed you desperately. You don't know what we've been through."

"I missed a connection in Chicago."

"Sit down, Doctor," interrupted Worrell. "There's something you should know."

Graves, looking puzzled, sat at the round table with the crochet cloth on it. From a sideboard Worrell brought an unusual-looking bottle and a glass and set them in front of the gray-haired man.

"A touch of whiskey?" said Worrell, uncorking the bottle. Graves raised his hand and gave a little smile. "A little too early—"

"Doctor," Worrell said suddenly, "Mrs. Barnaby was murdered."

Graves looked up at him in disbelief.

"Yes, murdered—poisoned—right here in this house," he almost shouted. "And whoever did it—God knows who it was— almost killed my mother too!"

"Murdered!" Graves passed his knuckles across his forehead. "God!" He sat quietly for a moment digesting the news. *Murdered!*

Then his hand went out to the bottle shakily. He took it and poured some of the brown liquid into the glass.

"Murdered," he breathed. "I can't believe it."

He started to raise the glass to his lips. Worrell quickly restrained his arm and took the glass from him.

"That's not whiskey, Doctor."

Graves looked at him uncomprehendingly. The doctor pulled the bottle closer and studied it.

42

"Liebig's Extract of Meat," he read aloud. Then he turned the bottle around and silently read the note glued on the back.

"What would you say, Doctor," said Worrell, "if I told you analysis has proved that bottle contained one hundred and thirty-two grains of arsenic?"

Almost as though answering a student's question in a classroom, Graves replied mechanically, "That could kill sixty-six persons." He held the bottle to his nose. "Who—who did it?"

"Someone who knew chemistry, obviously."

Graves kept smelling the bottle. "Probably arsenite of potassium. Any fool can make it—and one teaspoonful's fatal."

"My mother-in-law drank a whole glassful," said Laura Worrell, "and she recovered."

Graves shrugged. "Sometimes ingesting an overdose—say, ten grains or more—will cause a violent reaction. The victim will vomit and expel the poison. A smaller dose, on the other hand, may be absorbed and prove fatal."

Mrs. Allen turned to Mrs. Worrell exclaiming, "That's right; he's right, Florence! Remember, you said you took a big gulp and—and poor Josephine just kept sipping hers. Little sips."

"Why wasn't I notified? Why wasn't I told at once she'd been poisoned?"

"She thought she was getting better; she didn't want to trouble you."

Graves paced the floor. "Monstrous, utterly monstrous! The kindest of women. Who could have thought of killing her?"

And for the next hour they continued discussing the shocking crime, speculating as to the identity of the murderer and possible motives for the act. Worrell kept pressing Graves for any information he might have that could lead to any reasonable suspect, but the doctor was unable to believe anyone capable of such a heinous crime and became increasingly agitated.

"True, Bennett lived in the woods, so to speak, and they had quarreled—but murder! It's impossible. And her maid, Sallie Han-

43

ley—don't be ridiculous, Worrell! Sallie's a decent young woman. Certainly, she was put out with Josephine, but good Lord, man, do you realize what you're saying?"

"Dr. Graves," Worrell said quietly, "I don't wish to be rude, but why did it take you so long to get here? Two extra days?"

"I told you," Graves snapped, "I missed my connection! And felt I was coming down with the grippe; I stayed with an uncle in Sterling, Illinois. Besides, I knew she was dead—your last wire told me that. What could I do? What could anyone do for the poor woman? I knew nothing of—of—" he gestured angrily at the bottle. "There was nothing about this in the newspapers."

"We've managed to keep it out of the press so far. The autopsy— secret. We're taking her back to Providence for burial tonight. Her daughter arrived yesterday."

Graves raised his eyebrows. "Her daughter?"

"Mabel Conrad," said Mrs. Worrell. "She arrived yesterday. Staying at the Windsor."

Dr. Graves frowned. "I was under the impression that she disliked her mother."

"Dr. Graves," sniffed old Mrs. Allen, "I don't think that is an appropriate remark at a time like this."

"I'm sorry. I'm just upset. Terribly upset."

"She has asked that if you arrived to please have lunch with us all at the Windsor."

"How kind," Dr. Graves said. "I've got to see a friend first, then I'll call on her, directly."

"In any event, I'll see you at the train," said Mrs. Worrell.

As Graves started for the door, he said, "I'm—I'm stunned. Stunned by all of this." He looked around the room. "Forgive me if I'm not quite myself—I simply can't grasp all that happened. I've got to think—I must get some air. In the war and in my profession, death is an everyday happening. You get hardened. But not to a foul murder. And not to a friend."

Worrell followed him to the hall.

44

Mrs. Florence M. Worrell
The good companion

E. S. Worrell, Jr.
The suspicious son

"Dr. Graves, who besides yourself and us knew Mrs. Barnaby was going to be in Denver at this time?"

"I'm—not sure. She wrote from Pasadena and Del Monte but said only that she was going next to San Francisco."

"Try to think who would know that date, Doctor. You see, it is a relatively simple case to solve. The murderer was an idiot, a fool. The person who did this has to be among the handful of people who knew her exact plans."

"Let me think," said Graves. "Lord and Taylor in New York must have known. Her dressmaker. Who else? Sallie and the Bennetts. And, of course, her housekeeper Mrs. Hickey, and—I'll make a list later. My wife would know if she were only here. Kitty would know."

"Tomorrow John Howard Conrad's coming down from Montana, stopping on his way to Rhode Island for the funeral. He's in an insane rage—wild to track down the murderer of his mother-in-law. Says to hell with the expense. I wouldn't like that man on my trail."

"Nor I," said Graves. "Nor I, from what I've heard of him."

At the door Graves turned and looked back at the people in the room. "And I won't rest either until the murderer is brought to justice," he said. "You have my word." He put on his hat and coat, and the Swedish girl let him out.

Five

Graves did not go to the Windsor to lunch with Mabel Conrad. Instead he went to Tortoni's Restaurant with John Dalzell, manager of the Geometrical Wood Carving Company of Denver. He was a short, pleasant-faced man with a professorial mien. Graves had heroically saved the life of Dalzell's brother in the Civil War, and they were old friends. According to Dalzell, a highly respected person in the Denver community, this is what happened and what was said that afternoon.

After lunch they strolled around the city's streets, idly looking in the shops until train time, talking about mutual friends and mentioning the murder only briefly "because I could see that Tom was terribly upset. He also described a new medicine he was working on—he was absolutely sure it would do wonders for women in labor and in the actual act of childbirth."

Dalzell's testimony in court would include *almost* all of his and Graves' conversation. Much later—too late—he would break his silence, break the confidence, and reveal an intimate bit of the conversation which, had it been brought out in the trial, could very possibly have changed the result and altered the tragic course of the doctor's life. According to Dalzell, when asked about the two-day delay in his arrival, Graves said: "In spite of the death I saw and lived with during the war and in spite of the often morbid aspects of my profession, I have never been able to abide post mortems, funerals, wakes and the like. And Mrs. Barnaby was dead—I am a doctor, not an undertaker. All I could have done would have been to console the family, something I'm not good

47

at. And remember, she was a client and a friend—she was not a relative." He hesitated. "And—John—I must confess to you and only you. There was something else that kept me in Chicago." He smiled ruefully. "John—if you'd only seen her! I met her on the train to Chicago; well, I knew then that Mrs. Barnaby was dead and there was no need of me here and—well—it was quite a magical two days. But that is the end of it, I swear it."

Dalzell asked, "You won't be seeing the lady again?"

Graves shook his head. "Never. You know how I feel about my Kitty—I would never want to risk upsetting her, not in her state of health. Any emotional disturbance could be serious for her. No, Dalzell, it was just one of those things, a brief wonderful idyll which shouldn't have happened. But it did. She was a respected married woman from Oakdale, California, and all. I suppose I should feel guiltier than I do. But never again. The knowledge would destroy Kitty."

At the station the first person they saw in the depot was Mabel Conrad, surrounded by four elegant Louis Vuitton suitcases. At thirty-two my grandmother was far handsomer than her mother had been. She gave the impression of being a chic, titled English-woman. My mother wrote of her:

> My mother-in-law had great taste and her large house was filled with lovely furniture and objets d'art brought from Europe. She liked the social life and entertained charmingly. While not really beautiful, her carriage and bearing gave the impression of a handsome woman of elegance. I remember she had a mannerism—the expression "phew" which she said always quietly with pursed lips. This was used to indicate any number of reactions to any number of situations!

The description is an accurate one of Mabel Barnaby Conrad at a later period. But at this particular time of her life she was a nervous and discontented woman, and her eyes and mouth revealed it. Primarily she was unhappy with her seven-year marriage; John Howard Conrad was too much like her father—too busy with his mines and cattle and stores and politics and women to pay much attention to a wife. She loved her three children, but servants took care of them for the most part. Mabel was bored with her life. Montana in general, and Helena in particular, seemed very primitive, and the social life extremely provincial. Even though she lived in a mansion with every possible luxury, she yearned for a different milieu. Before her marriage she had lived in Paris, and she longed to go back for good. But Conrad had no intention of leaving lucrative Montana, especially since he was deep in plans to run for governor of the state. To relieve her increasing boredom, Mabel had been taking a succession of lovers, including Joseph Baker, her husband's business partner and brother-in-law. An ugly, name-calling, publicized divorce—a rare, shocking thing in those times—was only a year away.

Dr. Graves immediately recognized Mabel Conrad from photos Mrs. Barnaby had shown him. He introduced himself and Dalzell, expressing regret that he had not been able to lunch with her, and added: "Your mother was a friend to me, a good friend. How very much you look like her!"

Mabel Conrad murmured her thanks, said she was sorry he hadn't managed to come for lunch, and then turned aloofly to rejoin the Worrells.

"Well," said Dalzell, lighting a cigar, "not the warmest greeting in the world."

"She blames me entirely for the lawsuit," said Graves.

He then told his friend that Jerothmul Barnaby had left his widow an annual income of only $2,500 a year, a minuscule part of the legacy. Barnaby had justified this by claiming that his widow "would be too flighty to handle a substantial sum of money." Mrs. Barnaby had consulted Graves a week after the funeral and asked his opinion. Graves had thought it very unfair and advised her, if necessary, to threaten to sue the Conrads and her other daughter for a fair share. She did, and was awarded a substantial amount of money and property. Never especially close to her daughters, Mrs. Barnaby became completely estranged from them at this time.

"Josephine always referred to Mabel as the Dragon," said Graves.

"You sure that's all?" Dalzell asked, watching Mabel chatting with the Worrells.

"You mean because I didn't get to Denver sooner?"

"Maybe I'm wrong, but it was almost as though you had something to do with the murder."

Graves smiled. "Even the Dragon couldn't think that of me. And as for Mrs. Worrell, if anyone might be suspected, it's she."

He told how Mrs. Barnaby had informed Mrs. Worrell that she was included in the will for ten thousand dollars, and how desperately Mrs. Worrell needed that money. Her husband had once been wealthy, but he had lost everything a few years earlier and now was reduced to working as a clerk in a department store in Chester, Pennsylvania. Along with the money, they had lost the social standing that had meant so much to Mrs. Worrell. Ten thousand dollars would have seemed an enormous amount to her.

"Why would she have drunk the poison," asked Dalzell, "if she were the murderess?"

"She *says* she drank it," said Graves.

"But she was very sick—"

"Easily faked," said Graves, "and she looks remarkably well now."

"But the poison was sent from Boston."

Dalzell's voice trailed off when they saw through the window of the depot a wagon being wheeled toward the baggage car of the train; on it was a silver-gray coffin. It went by and was gone in a moment, but it was some moments before Graves answered, and when he did he had tears in his eyes.

"Dalzell," he said, "I'm going to find out who did this thing."

50

He collected himself. "The *bottle* was sent from Boston. Maybe the poison was added here in Denver. Or maybe Mrs. Worrell is in cahoots with her husband or with Bennett and one of them sent it from the East. Mrs. Barnaby told Bennett he was in her will also. He could have sent it, and Mrs. Worrell saw to it that Josephine drank it."

Then, as the stationmaster called out "all aboard," Graves added: "Don't worry, old friend, we'll get to the bottom of this. And of course, John—forget what I told you—about—you know—Chicago. I have your word of honor?"

The old friends clasped hands warmly.

Once on the train Mrs. Conrad and Mrs. Worrell spoke to Dr. Graves only when they encountered one another in the aisles or in the dining car. For his part Graves went out of his way to inquire after Mrs. Worrell's health and to ask Mrs. Conrad if he could do anything for her. The first morning, at breakfast, Mrs. Worrell complained of not feeling well and she leaned across the aisle to ask Dr. Graves if he had any medicine on board. He apologized for not having brought along his regular medical satchel but added that he did "have a small kit back in my compartment with some whiskey in it." At that, Mrs. Worrell threw up her hands, exclaiming "Don't mention that word to me!" and left the dining car and an embarrassed Dr. Graves.

That afternoon, at one of the stops, newspapers were brought on board the train. For the first time, a week after her death, the press told of Mrs. Barnaby's murder—and they told about it with relish in big headlines and stories that filled almost the entire front page. Everyone on the train read the lurid account with fascination.

By the time the train arrived in Jersey City on Sunday afternoon, the newspapers had had several days to speculate. On the platform a dozen reporters, plus sketch artists, swarmed around the principals of the drama, calling out their questions and embroidering the answers.

"Who's the Friend in the Woods?" asked a reporter.

51

"People are saying it was a Denver job," one reporter shouted at Mrs. Worrell. "What do you say to that?"

"Is it true, Mrs. Conrad, that you and your mother hadn't spoken for years?" asked another.

The women did their best to ignore the questions.

The New York *Times* reporter asked Dr. Graves: "Doctor, there are rumors that you are mentioned in the will for fifty thousand dollars."

Graves, impatient with the badgering, said, "I have no idea whether or not I am mentioned in Mrs. Barnaby's will."

"Not even for ten thousand dollars?" the reporter pursued.

"Look this way, Doctor!" said an artist, his sketch board propped against his stomach.

"For one thousand, or one hundred thousand, or for nothing," retorted Graves angrily. "Can't you believe that I simply do not know? I was not her lawyer!"

At that moment the baggage wagon with Mrs. Barnaby's coffin on it was pulled by. As was traditional, the reporters doffed their hats and held them over their hearts. Graves seized the opportunity to grab his suticase and race for the ferry. He made it just in time, and at Grand Central Station he caught the connecting train to Rhode Island; the rest of the funeral party did not.

Graves arrived at his home at 260 Benefit Street, Providence, at eleven that night. A tall man with a cadaverously thin face and rimless glasses approached the doctor from the shadows as he alighted from the cab in the glare of the street lamp. He identified himself with the Dickensian name of Henry Trickey, a reporter for the Boston *Globe*. Pulling a pad and pencil from his pocket, he said in a confidential tone:

"Doctor, in your opinion, who did it?"

"I don't know, Mr. Trickey, but I intend to find out, I assure you of that."

"How about Mrs. Worrell? How come she drank the poison and is perfectly fine? Did she fake it?"

"Nausea is easily feigned," said Graves, paying the driver.

"Doctor, just between us, more and more people are claiming that you had the most to gain by Mrs. Barnaby's death. What do you say to that?"

Dr. Graves snapped, "I say more and more people ought to mind their own business."

"Then you deny any implication in the—the unpleasantness?"

"Mr. Trickey, be logical. A large part of my income came from handling Mrs. Barnaby's business interests, to say nothing of taking care of her health. I'd have the most to lose by her death."

Dr. Graves tried to push past Trickey toward the gate in the picket fence which surrounded his house.

"So you never sent a bottle to Mrs. Barnaby?" persisted Trickey.

"I have sent a great many bottles to Mrs. Barnaby," said Graves. "None, however, containing poison. Good night."

The newspaperman stood blocking the gate. "Is that all you have to say to my readers?"

"Damn your readers," said Graves. "Stand aside—I wish to see my wife."

"You should have more respect for the press, sir," snapped Trickey as Graves forced himself by the man.

"And you should have more respect for individuals," Graves hurled over his shoulder as he entered his house.

Graves expected to be greeted by his adored wife, but instead his seventy-five-year-old mother met him with surprise. She showed him a telegram received earlier that day signed with his name:

RETURNING SUNDAY NIGHT. MEET ME AT YOUR BROTHER'S
IN DANIELSONVILLE.

"*They* did this!" he exclaimed, crumpling the telegram in his fist. "Those damned newspaper people. They've decoyed Kitty to Connecticut!"

He stormed out of the house and strode down the hill to the Western Union telegaph office. Lounging at the counter was Henry Trickey and his cohort, a self-styled private detective named Edwin McHenry. Upon seeing Trickey the doctor blew up. While there is some question about the exact conversation that was exchanged during this encounter, there is no doubt about the fact that Graves lost his temper. According to his testimony he shouted:

"What have you done with my wife?" He pushed Trickey aside. "Why did you do this? I'll use a horsewhip on the person who did it!"

"Doctor, tell us about Josephine Barnaby," countered Trickey. "What was that nice little lady *really* like? Isn't it true that she had a very interesting and busy private life? When you come right down to it, wasn't she pretty vile?"

"Vile?" said Graves, taking a yellow telegraph blank from the rack. He forced himself to calm down. "Vile?"

"She drank a great deal," said Trickey. "We all know that."

"She enjoyed a drink as many other people do," said Graves, taking out his pen. "Now please let me wire my wife."

"And what about her carryings on in the Adirondacks with Ed Bennett, the guide?"

"Mrs. Barnaby's private life was no concern of mine," said Graves, concentrating on what he was writing.

"Wouldn't you say it was pretty vile to carry on in an icehouse, drunk and with a married man?" said Trickey. "Couldn't someone blackmail her for that?"

Graves didn't answer and continued to write his telegram.

"Doctor," said Trickey, "supposing somebody had looked through a crack in the icehouse and was blackmailing her for her conduct and she failed to pay off—isn't it possible that then the blackmailer could have killed her? Isn't that possible, Doctor? Isn't it?"

"I suppose so," said Graves absently as he finished his telegram

54

T. Thatcher Graves, M.D.
The convicted murderer

Emma "Kitty" Graves
The long-suffering wife

and handed it to the operator in the green eyeshade. "How much do I owe you for that, sir?"

"So you agree that she was a vile woman?" said Trickey. "Really almost a whore?"

Graves turned exasperatedly: "What the hell do you want me to say? Something sensational? Something like 'she was a vile woman with vile lovers and a vile craving for drink' in order to satisfy the perverted thirst of your cheap newspaper? I can tell you she was anything but vile to me! And that is all I will tell you! Goodnight, Mr. Trickey."

But Trickey kept asking questions about Mrs. Barnaby, the Conrads, and the Worrells. And the next day the reporter's account of the conversation appeared in several versions on the front page of every major American newspaper. A portion follows:

> Dr. Graves stated that he thought Mrs. Barnaby had had to pay blackmail money and probably that she had refused someone hush money and the disappointed person had killed her. Also said that Mrs. Worrell was a coarse woman who was not so sick as she pretended. . . .
>
> He said he was sorry he'd ever met Mrs. Barnaby, said she was a vile woman with vile lovers, said he and his wife had been with Mrs. Barnaby in the Adirondacks the previous summer, and that she and the guide, Mr. Bennett, drank a great deal and that one day looking through a crack in the icehouse he saw the two lying drunk on the floor in the sawdust with every indication of a previous *revolting transaction* having taken place. This reporter suggested then that Mrs. Barnaby must have been a w———. Graves said that's right—she was a d——— w———. He and his wife left the Adirondacks disgusted. He said he had plenty more secrets about Mrs. Barnaby as well as her daughters and son-in-law, if he

but chose to tell them, and that people were wrong to
look to himself for a solution to the murder.

Yes, Mr. Henry G. Trickey had gotten himself a scoop and all
over America people were suddenly familiar with the name T.
Thatcher Graves. A shocking report in an era when even a glimpse
of a lady's booted ankle was considered racy, when Stanford White's
new Madison Square Garden was causing a scandal because of its
statue of Diana naked to the waist, which caused men to rent
binoculars from hawkers for a titillating look. The newspaper article
was highly damaging to the doctor; most readers chose to believe
that the reporter had quoted him accurately. Was this the way,
they said indignantly about Graves, that a loyal and honest doctor
would talk about his deceased benefactress and friend? Maybe—
could it be possible—that he knew more than he was telling about
the murder? Was it even conceivable that he himself had sent the
lethal bottle?

Unfortunately the public did not know at this time the true
character of Henry Trickey and his detective friend, both of whom
were to play a prominent and nefarious part not only in this case
but a year and a half later in the Lizzie Borden murders.

Messrs. Trickey and McHenry were dangerous enemies to have
against one, and they most surely were against T. Thatcher Graves.
The doctor read the newspaper account and was horrified. He first
wrote a scathing letter to Trickey and then a letter of total denial
to the *Globe*. Then he wrote to Mabel Conrad, who was in residence at her late mother's mansion across town at Sutton and
Broadway.

I am distressed beyond belief at the wild distortions and
statements attributed to me today in the newspapers. It
is true that I was emotionally upset and agitated to a
point of insanity by the press' having tricked my wife
away from our home and by their terrible accusations,

56

and I must have been betrayed into saying some rash statements—but I never uttered ninety percent of the things they claim and would never wish to sully the name of your mother in print or cause her family pain. I beg your forgiveness.

Graves' wife returned from Connecticut that day. It was never learned who had sent the false telegram or for what purpose she was decoyed out of Rhode Island.

With his wife back home, Graves recovered his poise, and when two reporters came to the door of his house, he invited them in to tea. Standing in front of the fireplace with his arms around his petite wife, Graves calmly admitted that he had had a great row with Trickey, said some things he had regretted, but in the main refuted most of that reporter's statements in a highly convincing fashion. The newspapermen, rivals of Trickey's, took it all down avidly, eager to exonerate Graves and discredit the competition.

Pretty Kitty Graves charmed the reporters as she poured tea from a silver pot. She was a frail brunette of thirty with haunted green eyes the color of her emerald ring, a flashing smile and a nervous but engaging laugh. She was from Connecticut of a substantial middle-class family, and her parents had brought her to Dr. Graves as a beautiful, disturbed eighteen-year-old girl. She had a history of mental trouble—shortly before she had been found totally nude in a meadow at midnight, babbling lines of Ophelia from *Hamlet*. Dr. Graves treated her for various nervous disorders and she appeared to regain her health in a remarkably short time under his care. After a year she and the doctor were married. There were no children, a bitter disappointment to her.

Inevitably, the reporters asked Graves who he thought had committed the murder. Graves said politely that there were so many possibilities it was hard to say, that it really was up to the police to do the guessing.

One of the reporters cleared his throat and said: "Excuse me

57

ma'am—but some folks are saying that—well, that your husband might have done this terrible thing—what do you say to that?"

Graves jumped up.

Kitty Graves' teacup rattled in her hand only slightly. Then she said vehemently but coolly: "I say that he could not and would not—and did not do it."

There was a brief silence. Then Graves burst forth. "Now listen, you sons of bitches, one more question like that to my wife and I'll personally throw you out of here! You are supposed to be intelligent people—use your heads, please! If I were bent on murdering Mrs. Barnaby—give me some credit—why would I send a bottle of poisoned water, not even poison in whiskey, not even in a whiskey bottle, not even colored to look like whiskey—why? Why to a house where a half dozen people might have drunk it before Mrs. Barnaby? Why 'Happy New Year' four months later? Why enough poison to kill a squadron when a small pill would have done it? And why not wait a week? She would have been home in a week—why not wait until her bimonthly checkup, inject an air bubble in her veins, and say she had a stroke?"

Mrs. Graves tugged his coat. Fuming, he sat down and struggled to regain his composure. To break the ice, one of the reporters handed Dr. Graves the latest edition of the Providence *Journal*. There were two separate stories on the front page. The one on the left proclaimed:

EXPERTS DECLARE HANDWRITING ON BOTTLE
DEFINITELY FEMALE!

"That doesn't look too good for Mrs. Worrell," commented one reporter.

"Or Sallie Hanley," said the other.

Graves didn't answer. He barely glanced at the newspaper and saw the other headlined column.

58

MRS. BARNABY LEFT TWO WILLS!
Lawyers Due to Open Tomorrow
Murderer Probably One of Those
Mentioned, Theorize Police

Shortly after the reporters left, a brisk rap of the brass knocker was heard. Expecting more newspapermen, Graves went angrily to the door. He opened it warily. There before him stood a sun-tanned, thick-necked, rugged man of thirty-six. Although attired in an expensive English suit and a foulard tie, he wore a modified Stetson hat and cowboy boots. With his moustache and teeth, he did not look unlike Teddy Roosevelt, and when his mouth widened it seemed more of an involuntary muscular spasm than a smile.

"Graves, I'd like to talk to you," he said, holding out his large hand. "Name's John Howard Conrad—Montana."

Six

Did my grandfather, John Howard Conrad, honestly believe that Thomas Thatcher Graves was the murderer of his mother-in-law? There is no way of knowing for sure. But what *is* certain is that he was out to pin the crime on the doctor from the outset: Graves had lost Conrad a great deal of money, and he was not about to forget it or forgive it.

Totally unsuspecting, Graves was taken in by this man's seemingly friendly and confidential manner and the cordial invitation to the Barnaby home. No two men could have been more different—the sophisticated intellectual Easterner and the blunt, rugged Westerner. As the two men got into the waiting carriage, Conrad said, "By God, Graves, I like a man who is manly enough to apologize for a wrong! Not that we believed that you ever said any of that junk in the papers. But your letter meant a lot to my wife. She wants to thank you in person."

The two men theorized about the murder motive, speculating on the possible murderer as the carriage rolled through the darkening streets, the prize-winning bays in their smart trappings needed no guidance from the coachman as they headed home at a fast clip. At the corner of Broadway and Sutton, a Negro youth was waiting in front of the ornate stable door and opened it to admit the carriage.

The Barnaby mansion, gabled, turreted and towered, was—and still is—a remarkable structure. The gingerbread stable alone runs from one block to the next and is quite unlike other stables of the times, being more like a French manor than a housing for harness horses. John Howard Conrad and Mabel Barnaby had celebrated their wedding in this stable seven years before. The day after that event a long article in the Providence *Journal* gave a gaudy account of the ostentatious affair, and for a baroque reportage it is likely to remain unrivaled:

THE MOST MAGNIFICENT SOCIAL EVENT FOR A SCORE OF YEARS
A PROVIDENCE BELLE MARRIED TO A WESTERN MILLIONAIRE
Presents Valued at $50,000 Besides $50,000 in Bonds
Mr. Barnaby's Princely Hospitality Enjoyed
by a Thousand People

The social event of the year has come and gone, our society belles and beaux have nothing more to think of, and Providence will become quiet again for a while. Rhode Island has seen wedding after wedding but nothing to equal the magnificence of last evening. The occasion was the nuptials of John Howard Conrad, a dealer in general merchandise with five establishments in Wyoming territory, vast holdings in Montana, a bank at Buffalo, two large houses in Chicago, and also the largest cattle owner in the northwest, a man with an income of $150,000 and capital of $4,000,000; and Mabel Barnaby, eldest daughter of Mr. and Mrs. Jerothmul Bowers Barnaby. . . .

Seldom, if ever, has a more regal looking or more finely dressed bride walked up the aisle of "Old Grace." On her fair neck flashed and glittered a necklace of diamonds and pearls, a gift from her father (valued at $25,000). . . . After the ceremony the hundreds of carriages headed for the bride's late home.

The house and stables were turned into bowers of beauty. Nature loaned her choicest beauties for this event and the wondrous perfumes of the buds and blossoms seemed almost as if made to order for the occasion. The

62

stable had been turned into a fairyland, a grand banqueting hall, the stalls' posts, frames, etc., all draped and twined with smilax, pointed with white and scarlet pinks and ornamental plants of every rare kind filled the corners and niches. From all over the ceiling dozens and dozens of cages of exotic birds were suspended and the silver-throated songsters mingled their liquid notes most charmingly with the sweet strains of one of the three orchestras. On either side of the room the huge mirrors reflected back again and again the hundreds of candlelights, while a golden tongued crystal bell swung slowly from the center. An unbelievable fairy bower, it is safe to say that a more beautiful vision was never arranged for mortal eyes to look upon.

Exactly at nine-thirty, Colonel Winship blew a whistle.

"Look—the ceiling is falling!" cried the astonished guests. Before their very eyes, seemingly by magic, a great portion of the ceiling was lowered steadily down, a gigantic table upon which were, besides magnificent candelabra and decorations, every type of succulent food known to man, charmingly displayed. Immediately twelve waiters, carefully trained in New York, sprang forth to serve the thousand eager guests....

It goes on for pages to describe—and to appraise like an insurance adjuster—every gift on display and pinpoint the giver, including "a $27,000 diamond bracelet from the groom."

Mabel Barnaby Conrad was wearing the same bracelet this evening as she greeted Dr. Graves in the foyer of the main house. It was an exceptionally warm greeting, or so it seemed to Dr. Graves after the chilly meeting in the Denver railroad station. A butler took the doctor's hat and coat.

"How very good of you to write that letter, Doctor," Mabel

Conrad said, extending her hand. "I was terribly upset when I read the newspapers. Your letter did more than anything could have to raise my spirits."

They went into the large living room where Graves and his wife had frequently been entertained.

The room was so typical of the era as to be almost a caricature. Marble corinthian columns with plaster cherubs in the corners, dark oak furniture, an overstuffed sofa covered with a leopard skin throw rug, draped red velvet curtains drooping gold tassels, and here and there baroque stands bearing statuettes. One entire wall was smothered to the ceiling in murky European paintings encased in ornate gold frames. Around and about the room were bamboo jardinieres, easels displaying sentimental chromolithographs, large glass domes over wax flowers, vases filled with cattails and, over the great marble fireplace, a stuffed owl. On the inlaid grand piano, replete with a Manila shawl, was young Maud Barnaby's sheet music: "Throw Him Down, McCloskey," "A Hot Time in the Old Town" and "After the Ball."

After Dr. Graves and John Howard Conrad greeted Mabel Conrad, they talked for a short time of the murder in general terms and the three discussed the funeral arrangements. Then Mabel Conrad asked to be excused because she had a headache. After she went upstairs, Conrad put his hand on Dr. Graves' shoulder and said heartily:

"It's drinking time, doctor! Come into the library—I want you to meet my brother."

He led the way into the small paneled library. There, sipping whiskey and reading by the light of a kaleidoscopic Tiffany lamp, was a forty-year-old man with a small goatee and furtive eyes attired in a way that suggested southern landed gentry. He stood up as they came in.

"Dr. Graves, I want you to meet my brother Charles," said Conrad. "Up from Richmond."

"Well, Doctor, I'm certainly glad to make your acquaintance,"

Henry G. Trickey
The investigative snoop

John Howard Conrad
The Montana bloodhound

the man drawled in the tones of a southern gentleman. "Mighty glad."

The man was neither a gentleman nor a southerner, and though John Howard Conrad did have a brother, Charles, back in Montana, this was not he. The man was Orinton C. Hanscom, a Pinkerton agent who had been lucratively employed by John Conrad for the past three months; Conrad had previously hired him to shadow his wife, whom he suspected of infidelity. But a week ago he had shifted him to bigger game: T. Thatcher Graves for the crime of murder.

"Been reading this new book called *Black Beauty*," said Charles. "Brings home the plight of the cab horse in a terrible fashion. In Virginia we treat our horseflesh better, I can tell you."

Conrad went to the bar and poured two large drinks. He offered one to Graves, who declined it, saying that he had a great deal of neglected work to make up in the morning. Conrad continued to press the drink upon the doctor, who continued to decline it; Conrad finally ended by pouring the whiskey into his own glass.

Conrad immediately turned the conversation to the murder.

"I swear, one minute I think the Worrells did it and the next minute I think Ed Bennett did it. What do you think, Charles?"

"I'm inclined to favor the ladies," said Hanscom. "That is, Mrs. Worrell and Sallie Hanley. Poisoning has always been a woman's art."

Graves said, "The reading of the wills tomorrow should tell us more."

Conrad put down his glass. "Doctor, the newspaper was misinformed," he said. "The wills were opened today."

Graves looked at him with interest. "And?"

Conrad and Hanscom studied Graves as the former spoke. "In the second will—the one that counts—Bennett was mentioned for ten thousand. Mrs. Worrell was also mentioned for ten thousand."

"A lot of money," said Graves. "A great deal of money."

"Twice as much as my own children were left," said Conrad.

There was a silence. Then Conrad said, "You, doctor—you were mentioned for fifty thousand dollars in the first will. It was changed to twenty-five thousand in the second, the most recent will."

"Lord!"

Graves stood up and ran his fingers through his hair.

"This is extraordinary," he said. "Extraordinary."

"You mean—that the amount was lessened?" said Conrad.

"That I was mentioned at all!" said Graves. "It was generous, unbelievably generous. I don't know what to say."

"Surely you knew you were in her will," said Hanscom.

"I swear I did not," said Graves. "I'm staggered at the amount. That is almost as much as I inherited from my own father."

"But you were a friend of Colonel Ballou's—you recommended him to be Mrs. Barnaby's lawyer some time ago." (We will be hearing more about the infamous colonel-lawyer later.)

"He wouldn't reveal professional secrets to me any more than I would to him. Besides, he did not draw up her second will. Mr. Worrell had that done in Chester."

They discussed the implications of the legacy, while Conrad and Hanscom had several more drinks.

"Better watch out for Colonel Van Slyck," said Conrad. "The trust has appointed him future custodian of Mrs. Barnaby's estate. He's been implying—hell, he's come right out and said it—that you have squandered great quantities of her money—some seventy thousand in the last few months."

Graves stated emphatically that he had bought seventy thousand dollars' worth of reputable stocks and bonds for her recently and had them in a Boston bank. He urged Conrad to go with him to Boston the next day to see the certificates with his own eyes.

Graves left the house at midnight. The next morning, as scheduled, he and Conrad went to Boston and examined the stocks and other accounts, apparently to Conrad's complete satisfaction. That evening Graves was once again invited to the Barnaby mansion, the second of a series of strange interviews between Conrad, "his brother Charles," and Graves.

For what happened during those confrontations we must depend solely upon the cut-and-dried testimony given at the trial, since there are great discrepancies between the several versions. Graves, on the stand, gave his account with, as the newspapers stated, "fluency, deliberation, and directness, looking at the court straight in the eye... the long forefinger on his left hand occasionally pointing at the jury, his fist at intervals being brought down forcefully on the arm of his chair."

After some talk about Mrs. Barnaby's holdings that second evening, the subject changed to other fields:

Mr. Stevens (the district attorney): What did you talk about?

Dr. Graves: We talked principally that evening in relation to Mr. Conrad's life in Montana, of his ranch, of his mines, of his political aspirations.

Q. I want the whole conversation.

A. My recollection is that Mr. Conrad had made some happy hits in coal mining and at that time, according to his story, he was in trouble because his miners had struck, that it was costing a good deal and he was in a hurry to return to Montana; that he didn't want to stay; he wanted to get back and he wanted to get rid of the whole thing, get back home on account of this strike, and the fact that his business was suffering.

Q. What did he say about his political aspirations?

A. He said that he was determined to become governor of Montana; and then senator from Montana; that he was sure of being governor, and sure of being senator. He gave me the impression that he was the leader of his party; that no nomination could be made in Montana, without he saying that it should be: that he had spent $25,000 the year before; that he presumed he should spend a good many twenty-five thousands; that he had

67

the money and was perfectly ready and willing to do it. During the evening the subject was broached by Mr. Conrad that he believed the death of Mrs. Barnaby had been caused by accident, that somebody must have sent her a bottle of whiskey, and it either had been tampered with or in some way that he could not explain it had been changed. We all three discussed who could have had a hand in the poisoning. Edward Bennett's name was mentioned; I said I had no idea that Bennett had anything to do with it. Mr. Worrell's name was mentioned; I didn't know anything about the Worrells, but Mr. Conrad kept saying that he thought the Worrells knew more about it than they wanted to explain, spoke of the secrecy that had been shown, and many other things of that kind which would rather tend to throw suspicion upon the Worrells. As I knew nothing in relation to the Worrells, I could not join in it one way or the other. But we talked up to pretty near eleven o'clock.

Q. Doctor, I will ask you to state—(whirling and shouting and stabbing a finger)—whether or not during that Monday night you stated to Mr. Conrad that you had sent to Mrs. Barnaby a bottle of pure whiskey!

A. (Firmly, quietly) No sir, I did not.

Q. (Calming down with exaggeration) What was the nature of these interviews up to and including Monday night, as to their being friendly or otherwise?

A. They were most exceedingly friendly, as I supposed.

Q. Did you see any whiskey there Monday night?

A. Oh, yes, oh yes—they hit it pretty hard.

Q. Who did?

A. Mr. Conrad and Charles.

Q. Did you drink any Monday night?

A. No, sir.

Q. Did they ask you to drink Monday night?

A. Nothing beyond the ordinary politeness. I was asked in the ordinary polite manner.

Q. You say you *think* you left about eleven o'clock that night?

A. I think I did. I think I got home about eleven o'clock.

Q. What condition did you find Mr. Conrad in when you got there?

A. He appeared to be pretty full, pretty full.

Q. Intoxicated—is that what you mean, Doctor?

A. Yes, sir.

Q. Then why don't you say so, sir? Let us try to be precise here.

A. I always try to be precise, sir.

Q. Was Charles there that night?

A. Charles was there every night, in and out of the room. He would saunter in and saunter out. He appeared to be an elegant gentleman—

Q. Southern gentleman?

A. Yes, that was the character he was masquerading under at that time. I might add that he played it to perfection.

Q. Well, what was said when you got in there that night?

A. After we got in the room, John Conrad appeared. I supposed he was tight, but I have reason to suppose that he was not now.

Q. What happened then, Doctor?

A. Well, he accosted me as "You Goddamned old Puritan, you have got to take a drink now!" And I did take one.

Q. Well, what was said after that?

A. Mr. Conrad said his wife was sick and tired and

wanted to get back to her children, and that he was fed up with the whole business. After a while he confided to me that he would give $25,000 to any man that would say he sent a bottle of whiskey to Mrs. Barnaby.

Q. How much?

A. $25,000. I thought it was simply drunken talk. He asked me if I supposed Edward Bennett would agree to say that he had sent a bottle of whiskey to Mrs. Barnaby. I said I did not, that Edward Bennett was not that kind of man, that he might have his failings, but he would not go that far.

Q. Did he state why he wanted somebody to say that?

A. He said that his political prospects in Montana would be ruined unless he could go back to these different politicians and could say to them, "Gentlemen, this was all a mistake, the papers have made a mistake, Mrs. Barnaby was not murdered." Then he could go back to Montana, he could hush the whole scandal up, and he could go back clean and whole before his constituents, and that his prospects of being governor of Montana would not be ruined.

Q. Proceed.

A. Well, he finally became very confidential with me. He said to me, "Now, Doctor, you can help me out of this. You did send a bottle of whiskey to Mrs. Barnaby, didn't you?" I said, "How could I—I never sent a bottle of whiskey! I can't do that." And then he would take another tack, then we would talk about Montana, and he drank again and appeared to be quite under the influence of liquor—and finally he said to me, "Doctor, let's forget the whole thing! Come on to New York and let's go on a spree together!"

Q. Did you have any conversation with brother Charles Tuesday evening about a bottle of whiskey?

70

A. No, sir.

Q. Did he say anything to you—or you to him—on Tuesday night about your having sent a bottle of whiskey, or was the conversation all with Mr. Conrad?

A. I am under the impression it was all with Mr. Conrad that evening. Charles now and then would put in a word or hear some of it, but he wasn't in the room more than a quarter of all the time.

Q. Can you remember whether you said anything to brother Charles that night about sending this bottle of whiskey?

A. I told "brother Charles" that he must get that idea out of John Conrad's head fast! I said to Charles, "For God's sake, I never sent a bottle of whiskey, and you know it and I know it. I never did. You must get that idea out of your brother's head."

Q. Why didn't you go Wednesday night?

A. I had been very busy through the day and was tired and didn't go.

Q. What had you been doing that day, Doctor?

A. Among a great many things, about eleven o'clock a gentleman called at my house with another gentleman and said that he was Colonel Van Slyck, and said that he had been appointed custodian to receive the Barnaby property. He handed me a paper. I read it through and he said how soon, when would it be convenient for you, Dr. Graves, to turn over the property? I said, "Now." He was very much surprised, and he said, "Now?" and I said, "Right now."

Q. Did you turn it over that day?

A. Yes, sir.

Q. Tell what occurred between John Conrad and brother Charles and yourself Thursday night.

A. We got comfortably seated in the library, and as I

71

had come at the request of John Conrad to talk over the wills, I began talking about the Chester will and the Ballou will, and I felt a change in John Conrad's manner. I intuitively felt that there was a change in his feelings toward me. We talked in relation to the wills for some time. Then John Conrad said to me, "Now, Doctor, in relation to the bottle of whiskey which you said Tuesday night that you had sent." I interrupted, "No, John Conrad, I never said so!" "But you did." "No," I said, "you know I never said so!" Upon that he flew into a passion, or pretended to, and said, "You did!" I said, "No, sir, I didn't." He then controlled himself and sat down saying, "You certainly did say so Tuesday night!" I said, "Sir, if I'd said so I'd know it!" "But," he said, "you said you did! My brother Charles will swear to it, too." I said, "I never said so. I never sent a bottle of whiskey to Mrs. Barnaby." Then he dropped that tack and began to wheedle me. He said, "Now, Doctor, you must help me out of this. I want you to sign a paper." He was standing up at the time. On the shelf where the decanter had been on the previous evenings I noticed a paper, a sheet of paper. I didn't take it in my hand; he didn't take it in his hand, but he made a motion towards it as though he wanted me to sign it, a paper stating that I had sent a bottle of whiskey. He went on to say that it should not be used against me; he just wanted it to show to his brother politicians; he wanted to take it back to Montana; he would just take it back and show his brother politicians that a bottle of whiskey had been sent. He tried every art of persuasion to persuade me. Failing to persuade or coax me, he then proceeded to threaten me. He said, "If you don't sign the paper I will have you arrested." That made me mad and I said, "If you have me arrested for this—" I really don't remember my exact words; I presume he is correct when he said that I would dig up the scandals of the Barnaby family; I did say something to that effect or of that nature. He made me mad, damn mad, and I did say something of the kind. Whereupon he flew into a perfect passion like a mad bull and he raved and stormed about the room and kicked the furniture and swore if I didn't help him he would have me arrested and bring me in irons to Denver. He said, "The East is your country, the West is mine! If you are taken to Denver I will pack a jury on you, you will never have a fair trial—with my money I'll buy up a jury and you will be convicted anyway!"

(Great rustling in the courtroom)

Q. Did he say anything about newspapers?

A. He calmed down after a while. Then he started again and said, "Dr. Graves, I have given a twenty dollar bill to ten different reporters. The Boston *Herald* I have bought up body and soul—Henry Trickey is in my pocket—they all will do just as I tell them to do; the Boston *Herald* you know is one of the principal papers and it has a good deal of influence." He then tried in every way that he could to get me to sign the paper. I tried to pacify him and I said to him for the hundredth time, "Mr. Conrad, it is no use talking. I never shall say so in the world, for I never did. I can't help you out of this." Finally the words became so high between us that Charles Conrad came into the room and immediately after he entered he said, "Charles, didn't Dr. Graves say that he sent a bottle of whiskey?" Brother Charles said, "Yes he did." I said, "Oh, no—other bottles, medicines, but never whiskey!" For some reason or other John Conrad left the room. I said to him, "Charles Conrad, you've got to get this idea out of your brother's head!" John Conrad came back into the room and bellowed, "Doctor, which is best: for you to go to Denver in a palatial car with me, or go in irons? For we will both of us swear that you did say that you sent a bottle of whiskey to Mrs. Barnaby." I turned around to face them both, and I said, "You call yourselves Conrads of Virginia! So help me God, if you two men go to Denver and swear my life away, I would rather be the prisoner at the bar than be you Conrads of Virginia!" Then I said, "Now I propose to leave this house." Both of them tried to restrain me but I insisted on leaving the house, and I did leave the house."

And so Dr. Graves stalked out of the mansion, believing he had closed the subject and washed his hands of Conrad. But this modern day Javert was not about to lose his quarry, his Jean Valjean, so easily. The next morning Conrad telephoned Graves and apologized.

"Got carried away," he said. "Little too much whiskey. But I've just received a telegram from Denver that changes everything—we know who did it now! Yessir! Come on over tonight and we'll discuss it like men."

Graves was reluctant but finally agreed to return to the mansion at six.

Conrad had indeed received a telegram from Denver. But it was a phony. However, he had also received a small, interesting item from Denver which would prove to be a devastating bit of evidence against Graves.

Seven

The telegram was indeed a fake, a plot to trap Graves. But the envelope held genuine and invaluable evidence against the murderer, whoever he, or she, was.

One of the reasons Conrad had stopped in Denver on his way east was to try to find the wrapping paper in which the poisoned bottle had arrived. Criminology was in its infancy—even finger-printing, for example, was not universally respected—but it seemed logical that the paper and the container might contain important clues. My grandfather was disappointed to learn that the wrapping paper had been thrown away the day Mrs. Barnaby had opened the package in the office of Schermerhorn and Worrell.

Then ten days later came a letter with its important clue. It was from Frank Schermerhorn saying that he had remembered that he had fished the wrapping paper out of the wastebasket and torn off the stamps to give them to his ten-year-old son for his collection. The stamps, and their Boston postmark, were enclosed.

After telephoning Graves, Conrad immediately went to Boston on the remote possibility that some clerk in the post office might remember the sender. As it turned out, no one remembered the package or the sender, but as Conrad was about to leave, one of the clerks studied the fifteen-cent stamps.

"This package was mailed here," he said, "but the stamps weren't bought here. They couldn't have been bought here on March 30th— we've had none of these orange fifteen-cent Daniel Websters in stock since last year. They changed the orange Websters to blue Henry Clays last February 22nd. Special commemorative issue."

Conrad went back to Providence and said to Hanscom excitedly, "Have your men check every post office in New England and find out which still were selling orange Websters by March 30th!"

"But there must be at least five thousand offices!" said Hanscom. "Think of the expense—"

"To be exact, there are nine thousand, one-hundred and twenty-two post offices in New England," said Conrad, "and damn the expense!"

Hanscom delegated the tedious and routine post office check to several other men; he had more important work. He had already been to the Adirondacks and interviewed Edward Bennett and reported his interview to Conrad. The guide, he had said, had been cooperative. Bennett was a leathery-faced muscular man of forty-five—blunt, hard drinking, hard working, who supposedly cheated at cards and who wasn't above pleasuring the female guests of his resort regardless of their age and irrespective of the fact that he was married. But he denied any knowledge of Mrs. Barnaby's murder.

"Hell," he said, "would I be stupid enough to write 'from your friend in the woods,' living in the woods as I do?"

"Dr. Graves thinks you did it," lied Hanscom. "He says you knew you were mentioned in the will. That you needed that money desperately in your business."

"Why that bastard!" said Bennett. "Sure I can use that ten thousand—who couldn't—but I wouldn't kill anybody for that amount. And as for him—"

Then he told Hanscom how Mrs. Barnaby was prepared to buy property from him the previous summer for $4,000.

"But her secretary, that chippie Sallie Hanley, lets the Doc know and he writes a letter threatening to have a guardianship put over her like she was crazy if she buys the land."

"Well, she *was* pretty flighty about money," Hanscom said, leading Bennett on, "and the land was worthless, wasn't it?"

"Like hell—when she didn't buy it, when she wasn't allowed

Orinton M. Hanscom
The deceptive Pinkerton

Miss Sallie Henley
Mrs. Barnaby's saucy secretary

to buy it, I turned around and sold it for five thousand. I've got the papers to prove it."

Hanscom pumped him about Sallie Hanley.

"She was young, sexy—" said Bennett. "You should have seen how she rode a horse around—astride, like a man! Half-naked, breasts bouncing. She fell off her horse once and every man on the place was rushing to try to get a look before she got her skirts down."

"What did Mrs. Barnaby think of all this?"

"She was disgusted. Maybe jealous of the way Graves looked at Sallie. Yes, he was up here too for a couple of weeks. I'd like to punch him in the nose for what he said to the papers about me and Mrs. Barnaby. So would my wife, I can tell you."

"Was it true?"

"None of your beeswax, mister. The point is my wife thinks it was true after reading it in the paper."

"Mrs. Barnaby fired Sallie," said Hanscom. "Did she send that bottle?"

"She was plenty mad at Josephine," said Bennett, "and I heard she sent a threatening letter to her. But I don't know whether she killed her or not. The papers say it was a woman's writing."

"Maybe your wife sent the bottle," said Hanscom, "for fooling around in the icehouse."

Bennett's reply to this was not recorded.

Meanwhile, Hanscom's office had tracked down Sallie Hanley; she was working in a Providence dentist's office. Conrad went to see her alone since Hanscom was on his way to Chester, Pennsylvania, to talk to the Worrells. At first the pretty blond was surly and declined to talk about Mrs. Barnaby. When Conrad told her that her former employer had been murdered she expressed surprise and shock. Since the murder had been on the front page of every newspaper in the country for many days, it was hard to understand how she had managed to avoid reading about it.

"I never read the papers," she said.

77

She told Conrad that Graves had hired her to help Mrs. Barnaby, to write her letters for her, and to be a traveling companion.

"What about the threatening letter?" asked Conrad.

"Bennett must have told you that!" said Sallie. "Trying to get me in trouble, just because I wouldn't—you know—give in to him. Sure, I wrote her a letter! I was plenty mad when she fired me, calling me a hussy and worse names just because I'm young and the boys like me. Your mother-in-law wasn't perfect herself, I can tell you!"

"So you threatened to kill her?"

"I don't think I went that far—I just demanded three more months' salary, or else."

"Even though you were fired?"

"I deserved the money, God knows! What I went through!"

"And you threatened her life unless she sent the money?"

"I think I just said I'd—I'd do something to her."

"Like sending her a bottle of poison?"

"I never did it," said Sallie. "People don't always do things they say they'll do when they're mad."

"So who did do it?" asked Conrad. "Graves?"

"Dr. Graves!" exclaimed Sallie. "Never. Why he's the finest man I've ever known. I think it's the Worrells, like the newspaper said today."

"I thought you never read the papers," said Conrad as he put on his hat and left. He hurried back eagerly through the twilight to the Barnaby mansion to keep his appointment with Graves. With his new weapons, the phony telegram plus the rigged evening newspaper story, plus his conviction that neither Sallie nor Bennett was involved, plus whatever the stamp investigation would disclose, one can almost see him rubbing his hands in anticipation as he waited in the library, pacing up and down with his tumbler of whiskey. When a knock came on the door he sprang to open it even before the butler could get there.

* * *

78

Why this eagerness to convict Graves of the crime?

I never saw my grandfather (though I was six when he died in 1928) and it is difficult for me to be objective about him. First of all, I liked my father, a decent, gentle, humorous man. But he did not like his father and must have had good reasons. Secondly, when John Howard Conrad sued my grandmother for divorce in 1893 charging adultery, she countersued, charging him with adultery, drunkenness, neglect, cruelty and savage beatings. Since I did know her so well (she died when I was twenty), I am inclined to believe her charges. It would look as though he was inclined to physical solutions to problems even though he sometimes got the worse for wear.

It wasn't as though he were excessively fond of his mother-in-law and therefore sought to avenge her death; he had not bothered to see her for years, though he had been east frequently and she had been west. And it seems to me there was more to my grandfather's vengeance than the fact that he felt Graves had bilked him out of a great deal of money, consequently wounding the Conrad pride, demeaning him in his own eyes and in the eyes of W.G., his feared older brother. To partially understand Conrad and his vendetta against Graves, one has to understand the underlying rivalry, differences and suspicions that easterners held for westerners and vice versa. In those times East was East and West was still very much West; while parts of California were considered semicivilized by eastern standards, Montana was still looked upon as a rugged pioneer place, a foreign country. Montanans were looked down upon by easterners as mugget pluckers and cowpunchers in spite of whatever wealth they might have. After all, Montana had been a state for only two years, and Custer's massacre was only fifteen years old. Violence was still commonplace, and when in his native state Conrad usually packed a pistol; Billings and Missoula and Helena were not all that civilized yet, and would not be for some years to come. For example, a letter to me in 1969, from eighty-two-year-old Henry Johnston, a boyhood friend of my father's, recounts an incident that happened more than a decade after the death of Mrs. Barnaby:

In the spring of 1905 Ike Gravelle terrorized Montana and Wyoming. He was a throwback from Jesse James and the prototype of Dillinger. His favorite method of operation was to demand $25,000 from the Northern Pacific, in default of which he threatened to blow up a bridge or a station. Of course the railroad refused to pay tribute and he did considerable damage before he was caught. The courthouse was only a couple of blocks away from your great-uncle Dick Harlow's house and your dad and I attended every session. It was a sensational trial and we two impressionable teenagers got a big charge out of our proximity to one of the most dangerous desperadoes of the decade. The trial had ended on the fifth day, the judge adjourned for lunch and announced that he would charge the jury on reconvening. Barney and I went home and after luncheon returned to the courthouse. Just as we rounded the corner a fusillade of shots rang out. I can still hear them as they flew around our heads. We threw ourselves to the ground as we saw Ike, revolver in hand, running full speed across the square. It seemed a confederate had managed to put a gun in his hand as he was being brought into court. Ike shot and killed one of the deputies guarding him and wounded the other. When he ran out of the courthouse a horse was supposed to have been tethered for him nearby but something went wrong and there was no horse so he was forced to flee on foot. As he ran across the square every armed citizen, and there were many who carried guns in those days, took a pot shot at him. He was run to ground in the basement; the police rushed in and shortly

emerged carrying Ike's body. He had shot himself through
the head.

In 1891, Montana was an even more rugged place. The huge
state had a population of only 143,000, most of whom lived in the
western valleys. The plains to the east were more of a dangerous
hindrance to travelers than a haven for settlers. But the discovery
of gold, silver and copper—a gross wealth of some forty million
dollars in a short time—had made Montana a boom state for a few.

John Howard Conrad's older brother W. G. Conrad had been
in on the history of the state from the beginning. While John
Howard was dynamic and sought in every way to emulate his
brother, it appears he could never hope to equal ruthless, canny
old W.G., who had become a legend; the only place W.G. had
partially failed was in politics. Perhaps John Howard thought that
here was a way finally to top his brother, to become governor and
then senator—and Dr. Graves, with this scandal, had badly hurt
his chances. But by speedy "justice" he might turn the hurtful
murder case into helpful propaganda for the glory of the Conrad
name. And it *was* quite a name, I began to discover as I went
through the various accounts of the state.

Historian Dorothy Floerchinger of Conrad, Montana, has written:

> The history of Montana would not be complete without
> the story of the Conrad brothers, Charles, William G.
> and John Howard, and the vast financial empire they
> built. W.G. was the best known and it was for him that
> the town of Conrad was named. He was born August 3,
> 1848, one of thirteen children to Col. James and Maria
> Ashby Conrad. It seems fitting that a man who left such
> a deep imprint on the history of the state should have
> had for his birthplace such a historical spot as the Shen-

81

andoah Valley in Virginia. Soon after the close of the Civil War, which left their ancestral home in ruins, the two penniless brothers started west.

W.G. and Charles arrived in Fort Benton in 1868 and began clerking for I. G. Baker, trader and freighter of the American Fur Company, a thriving concern whose basic economy, lamentably and illegally, was based on exchanging furs for liquor with the Indians. The younger brother John Howard Conrad came west and joined them. Four years later they became Baker's partners and, in 1876, bought him out.

(About this time a young lawyer, William H. Hunt, fresh from Yale, started practice in a log cabin at the edge of town. After a few years he and John Howard Conrad both happened to move to Helena, where his daughter married Conrad's son and eventually became my parents. Hunt became Montana's first attorney general, Supreme Court judge and was governor of Puerto Rico from 1898 to 1904).

During the period 1868 to 1902, the brothers built a business empire that extended from New Orleans to the Great Slave Lake in the north. They sold goods all over the world, worth millions of dollars annually. In 1874, they freighted thirty million pounds of supplies to the Canadian government. The mercantile business had stores in Calgary, Fort McCleod, Lethbridge and Fort Walsh, which they sold to the Hudson's Bay Company in 1888. Their business years in Fort Benton lasted from 1872 through 1891.

In 1875 they bought the steamer *Red Cloud* and in 1876, with T. C. Powers, built the *Benton No. 2*. The Conrads also built the *Colonel McCleod*. These ran between Fort Benton and St. Louis, shipping annually 30,000 buffalo robes and $100,000 worth of fine furs. In 1879–80 they were the territory's largest freighters, employing 80 men, 576 oxen, 100 mules and more than 100 wagons. They freighted for the U.S. government and carried gold from the gold camps.

The Conrads also had cattle interests that extended from Great Falls into Canada. The Conrad Circle Cattle Company, with headquarters at Stanford, Montana, was capitalized at one million dollars, and at times there was a $70,000 payroll on the cattle ranches.

They also held timber interests in the Flathead Valley, Washington, Oregon and British Columbia. Other interests were the Queens Mining and Milling Company at Niehart and the Mantle Mine, Helena, an early-day sensation that produced over $500,000 from one shot. It was leased by W.G. and produced $103.89 per ton. A few years after the discovery of the fabulous placers of Last Chance Gulch (1864) the Spring Hill Mine was discovered. It contained an enormous deposit of gold ore which was later developed by W. G. Conrad. They had the Townsite Company in Kalispell (Montana's fourth largest city, started from scratch by Charles Conrad); Montana Life Insurance Company; Conrad Townsite Company of Conrad; a real estate company. At the time of W.G.'s death he owned the widespread Conrad Bank and held interests in five other banks.

A cartoon in a Great Falls newspaper once had this to say about W. G. Conrad in a caption:

Some millionaires run to fast horses,
Some of them run to the arts,
While some of them peddle the popping wine
To bring the warm blood to their hearts.
But art cuts no ice with your uncle.
I decline all the bubbles with thanks,
For my own little fad keeps me busy and glad,
I make a collection of banks.

John Howard Conrad was president of the fabulous Park Coal and Coke Company near Livingston, had the J. H. Conrad Bank of Red Lodge, owned a chain of several general stores in Montana and Wyoming, and subsequently struck it big in the Windy Arm mining district close to the headquarters of the Yukon. He sold his Alaska holdings alone in 1905 to W. McKenzie, owner of the Canadian Northern Railway, for five million dollars.

One history of Montana says:

> The second brother, Charles Conrad, seems to have been responsible for the business west of the mountains and in Canada, and in Kalispell he is remembered for his beautiful home where he and his wife entertained in the grand manner of the South. His private herd of bison became the nucleus of the National Bison herd at Moiese, Montana.
>
> But all of this fame and fortune did not prevent tragedy. Headlines in the Great Falls *Tribune* for November 26, 1906, were, "Body of Infant Is Stolen From Its Grave By Ghouls." Three-year-old son of Harfield Conrad, son of W.G., died of spinal meningitis. The body was stolen and held for ransom. Someone using the name of W. C. Hastings sent many notes that could not be traced. Negotiations came to a climax May 10, 1911, when Harfield and brother, Arthur, attempted to make contact with the body snatcher near Floweree. In the confusion, they shot and killed their friend, Sheriff Josephus Hamilton.

The Conrads, it would seem, attracted—or were attracted to—violence, and John Howard Conrad entered into his mother-in-law's murder case with enthusiasm. He seemed to think that to achieve his goal there was nothing wrong with entrapment, duplicity and feigning cordiality to a man he had every intention of sending to the gallows.

"My brother's not here yet," Conrad said to Graves, with his Teddy Roosevelt smile, "but I can't wait to show you what I've got!"

84

Graves entered the library warily, and refused the drink which Conrad proffered.

"You've been following the case in the newspaper this week," said Conrad, "about how the police are more and more convinced that the crime was committed in Denver?"

Conrad neglected to say that he had paid the newspaper a large sum to plant this story, which was written by reporters who were also paid large sums by him to write the lies.

"Now look at this!" Conrad handed a telegram to Graves. Datelined Denver, it read:

EVIDENCE CERTAIN POISON INTRODUCED INTO WHISKY BOTTLE AFTER ARRIVAL IN DENVER. INDICTMENT OF EDWARD WORRELL, JR. IN PREPARATION. NEED TESTIMONY OF DOCTOR GRAVES CONCERNING PHYSICAL CONDITION OF MRS. BARNABY PRIOR TO DEATH. PLEASE ASK HIM IF HE WILL COME TO DENVER TO GIVE DEPOSITION.

Although it was signed "Chief of Police," the telegram had been sent by the head of the Pinkerton Agency in Colorado, James McParlan, who was also in cahoots with Conrad.

Anyone familiar with the Molly Maguire hangings of twenty Irish Catholic miners, the nation's largest mass execution, in the wake of the tragic "Long Strike" of 1875, will remember the name of the controversial Pinkerton informer McParlan. Clarence Darrow exposed him as having turned perjured evidence, and Clancey Siegel, a biographer of the Wobblies, wrote that McParlan "was simply outside the human pale...a case of pure evil." In 1970, in the New Republic, Russell W. Gibbons wrote that "professional stool-pigeon McParlan's mentor was Franklin B. Gowen, the mine owner, railroad tycoon and political power who bought and paid for the Pinkertons and labor spies."

Now, sixteen years later, McParlan had a new tycoon to work

for—John Howard Conrad. And the pay was good. Conrad had another corruptible ally against Graves.

Graves handed the telegram back to Conrad.

"You see," said Conrad, "it wasn't Bennett or Sallie after all. You will go, of course?"

"My patients," protested Graves, "and the time and expense!"

"I insist upon paying your way and repaying you for your time," said Conrad.

Graves hesitated only a moment. "Justice must come first," he said. "I will go with you to do whatever I can. Let me tell my wife."

Conrad made plans to go to Denver that Friday. With them went Hanscom, who Graves still believed to be Charles Conrad. Before getting on the train, Hanscom, in private, was able to report to Conrad his amazing findings about the stamps: of the 9,122 New England post offices, only the Providence post office was still using the orange Websters. They had so little call for fifteen-cent denomination stamps that they still had a large supply of the old Websters. This meant only one thing to Conrad—the murderer had purchased the stamps in Providence, then journeyed to Boston to mail the package and thus divert suspicion from Rhode Island. And now he believed more than ever that the murderer was no one else but Graves.

Three days later, when Graves and his wife, followed by Conrad and Hanscom, stepped off the train at Denver, two police officers strode forward and greeted them. One of them said to the stunned doctor:

"Thomas Thatcher Graves—you are to be indicted for the murder of Mrs. Josephine Barnaby as soon as possible."

Conrad and Hanscom looked at each other and smiled.

Eight

And so the stage was set for one of the most sensational and longest murder trials America had yet known, the State of Colorado vs. T. Thatcher Graves, M.D.

The day after Graves arrived the Rocky Mountain *News* carried four major stories on its front page. On the left the heading read:

EDISON, THE WIZARD OF ELECTRICITY, HAS
PERFECTED A WONDERFUL APPARATUS
Applies for patent on a kinetoscopic camera
for taking motion pictures on a band of film
to be viewed by peeping into a box.

On the right side the headlines said:

PRESIDENT HARRISON TO VISIT US
First American President to Visit Denver

Below that appears:

APACHES ON WARPATH
Many Murders in Wilcox, Arizona Reported

And in the middle of the page in bold type:

HE IS HERE!
Dr. Graves in Denver. To be indicted.

District Attorney Stevens will not admit who the accomplice is. Said to be woman living in Denver.

Why, one may legitimately ask, so much excitement about the case, enough to overshadow a great invention, the arrival of a president, and Indians on a rampage? There were many peripheral elements about this very American murder that intrigued the un-jaded public of 1891; unheard-of things unmentioned in proper society, like mistresses, adultery, rifts in the sacred relationship between mother and daughters, the sullied trust between a patient and her doctor, the tarnishing of the career of a distinguished Army officer, the possible exposure of the darker side of a Harvard gentle-man, and the confrontation between East and West. For a society only one year away from the Ferris wheel, here was great enter-tainment and high drama. Criminology and private detectives and Pinkerton men were all so new and romantic. Thanks to Arthur Conan Doyle's recent books and stories, the public knew all about clues and magnifying glasses and "modern" detecting methods and exotic ways of murdering people.

And there was the added, exciting fillip of this being the first murder known to have been committed by mail. Others would later follow suit and emulate the murderer of Mrs. Barnaby by using the United States mails to kill.

In 1898, Roland B. Molineux was convicted in New York of killing two persons at two different times by sending a gift of Bromo Seltzer heavily laced with cyanide of mercury to his former fellow club members. Also in 1898, Mrs. Welcome A. Botkin sent arsenic-laden chocolates from San Francisco to Dover, Delaware, and mur-dered her lover's wife and her sister.

In 1906, an English gentleman named Thomas Mathieson Brown sent an iced shortcake loaded with strychnine to his uncle, which was intercepted by his unfortunate housekeeper, who ate it and subsequently died.

There have been other murders by mail, detected or undetected;

the most recent one occurred in Marshall, Michigan: one Enoch D. Chism was accused of having first mailed poison pills to his friend of twenty years, Mrs. Nola Puyear, and when she failed to take them, of sending her a bomb which killed her instantly.

In Denver, the district attorney, Isaac Stevens, proclaimed "this foul and dastardly poisoning of Mrs. Barnaby to be the very first murder by mail—probably in the world, and certainly in the United States of America. And now all of America is looking at Denver this moment in time to see how Colorado handles foul crime and wicked murderers—we will show them how swift and true is western justice!"

Dr. Graves arrived in Denver on May 12 and was indicted for murder on May 19, a month to the day after his alleged victim died. But even before his indictment the papers were full of gossip and innuendo, not all about Graves. The Rocky Mountain *News* reported:

> Both Sallie Hanley and Mrs. Graves are suspected. It is suspected that Mrs. Graves wrote the inscription on the bottle and that Sallie carried the poison to Boston, but the detectives have not found sufficient evidence to establish the fact yet. Miss Hanley, however, has been indicted. It is suspected that there was an improper and illegal relationship between Dr. Graves and Sallie.

Sallie was never indicted, though she was due to arrive in Denver in ten days.

The Providence *Telegram* ran a long, supposedly authentic interview with Dr. Graves' mother, describing her as "having a kind, motherly look, her head crowned with white hair, a tired and worried looking lady of sixty."

(With a fifty-year-old son, why wouldn't she look both tired and worried?)

Even the New York *Times* was not above repeating hearsay:

CHESTER, PENNSYLVANIA. The fact that Mrs. Worrell was poisoned from drinking what was supposed to be whiskey has caused considerable comment here where Mrs. Worrell has always been known as a strong temperance advocate.

The Boston *Globe* stated boldly on the front page:

The only motive that has been suggested for the crime here is revenge. There is in Boston a dressmaker who was discharged because she told a disagreeable story about Mrs. Conrad, Mrs. Barnaby's daughter, and a coachman.

Neither the coachman nor the dressmaker is mentioned again in the newspapers or at the trial.

It is hard to know what to believe among the spate of "reporting" in the newspapers of this time, though this, from the Denver *Times*, has the ring of truth to it:

Dr. Graves was indicted Saturday and he was arrested today. He spent his last day of freedom at his hotel. In spite of the fact that he is resting under a cloud, he has a good many friends in Denver who do not believe him guilty. He and his pretty wife have been guests of a number of prominent people in the city and have been the recipients of flowers from several people who are strangers to them but who sympathize with them in their difficulties. Dr. Graves told this reporter that he was glad that he was arrested, that he had expected it, and that it would give him a chance to vindicate himself: all he wanted was justice. He could not imagine why Sallie Hanley should be indicted but refused to say more about the girl. He seemed to be very upset about his wife, thought it very unfair to accuse his wife of having anything to do with the crime and that the insinuation had hurt him very much. After having been remanded by the court to jail to await trial, Dr. Graves was permitted to return to the Gilsey House for his valise containing clothing. His leavetaking of Mrs. Graves was a touching scene. He made a brave effort to appear calm and cool and made a handsome figure with his military bearing. Mrs. Graves, taking him by the hand, said:

"Now keep up your courage, Tom. You know, and we all know, that you are innocent and the Lord will be with you."

Without a second's warning the big man seemed suddenly to lose all his strength. He staggered a little, and then as a glass of water was handed to him he completely regained his composure and strode out with the deputy sheriff, his head held high. Almost immediately after he left, Mrs. Graves, overcome, sank on the lounge in a fainting spell.

Nine

Colorado in 1891 was proud of its new execution chamber, a place to which John Howard Conrad and the prosecution earnestly desired to present T. Thatcher Graves a one-way ticket.

Technically, it was a do-it-yourself hanging machine—no hangman need apply. The prisoner simply stepped out on the trap and did the dirty work himself—no fuss, no mess, no guilt for the lawmakers. (I savor the last words of an Englishman, William Palmer, who in 1856 was convicted of a poison murder. On the scaffold, when ordered to step out on the trap, he inquired: "D'ye think it's safe?")

Here is a contemporary description of it, and one wonders what early Rube Goldberg invented it and why it never caught on with other penal institutions:

> The execution chamber is constructed of stone, and is situated within the prison wall, just behind the cells.
>
> The chamber, or house, is about fifty feet in length by about fourteen in width, and is ten feet high.
>
> Entrance is effected through a single door. A brick partition divides the place into two rooms.
>
> No man hangs a criminal in Colorado: the condemned man commits suicide without his knowledge, which result is brought about by a novel device.
>
> A small space in the floor of the large execution room is raised about one quarter of an inch by means of springs. Over this hangs the noose, which is conducted by a

system of pulleys into the rear room, and is attached there to a 500-pound weight, which is held in place by a delicate trip lever.

On the lever is suspended a vessel holding fifty-six pounds of water.

When a murderer steps under the noose his weight on the small platform causes it to sink. In doing so it presses on a rod, which is in turn connected with a chain attached to a plug in the bottom of the water vessel.

This starts the water running, and when the tank is lightened fifty-six pounds the lever is suddenly forced up by a spring, the weight drops, and the murderer is jerked five feet in the air.

On the wall in the death chamber is a white disc about eight inches in diameter, across which a red line is drawn.

A black hand or dial starts on its journey around the disc as soon as the water is released, so that the witnesses to the execution in the front room know the exact second the weight will drop, when the black hand touches the red mark.

This device has been used in the Colorado penitentiary ever since the secret law went into effect, and in no case has it ever failed to break the neck of the condemned, who are launched into the other world while the chaplain is reading the service.

(Other accounts state it had never been used before and that Dr. Graves was to be the guinea pig.)

So neat and blameless, such a civilized way to eliminate an impeccable, Harvard medical man indicted for murder.

But even Conrad had to admit that first the doctor had to be *proved* a murderer, and that, perforce, would necessitate the formality of the trial in the spirit of American jurisprudence.

94

Selecting a jury was an unusually long procedure, and the preliminaries had their own little drama.

At ten o'clock the defendant appeared in court, accompanied by his counsel, Messrs. Macon and Furman of Denver and Col. Daniel E. Ballou of Providence, and took a conspicuous seat in the front row of chairs reserved for the jurors. After a glance about the room, which convinced him that he was "the observed of all observers," he settled back in his chair and gave undivided attention to the arguments.

And a real argument started right off the bat between the opposing attorneys. The court transcript reported:

"Mr. Furman, do you mean to say that I entered into a positive agreement as to the time when a list of these witnesses should be served upon you?" asked District Attorney Stevens.

"I do," replied Mr. Furman, "and the affidavit of Judge Macon bears out the statement."

"It's an infamous lie!" declared Mr. Stevens angrily.

"Oh, just wait till we get into this trial and I'll make you squirm," retorted Mr. Furman, violently shaking his index finger at the district attorney.

"Now, your honor," said Mr. Stevens, "if this case is to be tried on these disgusting personalities, I don't want to be associated with it."

"See the galled jade wince!" taunted Mr. Furman.

"Never do you mind about the wincing," was Mr. Stevens' rejoinder, "before you get through with this case we will see who winces the most. No attorney I've ever met from Texas has made me wince any!"

"Gentlemen, let this quarreling stop this instant!" commanded the court. "I will not permit it and you might as well understand it first as last. I hope I shall not have to speak of it again!"

The preliminary fireworks over, there followed a dramatic and impressive scene. Clerk Cobbey arose, unrolled the indictment

95

and facing the accused said clearly, "T. Thatcher Graves, stand up and be arraigned." The doctor obeyed and the Clerk Cobbey slowly read the indictment, formulated in three counts.

During the reading, which occupied about ten minutes, Graves' eyes occasionally wandered from floor to ceiling. The reading completed, Clerk Cobbey asked formally, "What is your plea to this indictment, guilty or not guilty?"

There was a deathly stillness in the courtroom. A newspaper report went all out in describing the scene:

> It was a moment freighted with the most significant import to one accused of a ghastly crime. He stepped forward four paces, directed his eyes unflinchingly to the court, and, making a respectful obeisance, replied with measured and distinct emphasis on the last two words: "May it please your honor, I am not guilty."
>
> He stood as motionless as a statue, reminding one of the pen pictures of Napoleon at Helena, where he is described as "standing with his hands behind him gazing out upon the sad and solemn sea." He was apparently upon the point of adding something, and everyone leaned forward and in hushed expectancy awaited his utterance. Counsel Furman quickly interrupted, "That will do, sit down, Doctor." The defendant mechanically turned and resumed his seat behind his counsel, wiping the perspiration from his face in his nervous agitation. The battle for his life had begun.

The following ten days were occupied in selecting a jury—some five hundred people were screened—and finally, on December 2, twelve men were impaneled. They were a hardware salesman, a contractor, a liquor salesman, a gunsmith, a hotel clerk, a farmer, two cabinetmakers, a miller, a real estate salesman, a timekeeper and a retired gentleman. None had been born in Colorado, showing what a young state it was. All were from the East except for one from England and one from Germany. All but one wore moustaches or beards.

Apropos of none of the jury being originally from Denver, we have to keep reminding ourselves how young Denver was at this time, in spite of its grand opera house, its great mansions, its parks and its imposing capitol building with its gold leaf dome.

The statehood of Colorado dated from only fifteen years earlier.

Denver was founded in what was called the "Pikes Peak or Bust!" gold rush of 1859. The site had been a stopping place for Indians, fur trappers, traders and explorers. Then came the discovery of gold, and 150,000 gold-bedazzled people streamed across the plains. Denver was named after the governor of the territory, James W. Denver, and it became the official capital of the territory in 1867.

At first gold wasn't found in great quantities and many Pike's Peakers slunk home as "gobacks." But just as it appeared that Denver would be depopulated by a reverse rush, great new strikes were discovered. Then the coming of the railroads in 1870 furthered the city's boom. In 1870 the population was 4,700; twenty years later it had grown to 157,000.

Besides the gold, great veins of silver were found and millionaires were created overnight. Their world would crumble in 1893 with the great Silver Panic, but right now in 1891, all was glitter, all was opulence in Denver. For example, the opera house:

Horace Tabor, an ignorant man from Kansas who had stumbled across several silver lodes and was now a multimillionaire—and soon to become Senator Tabor for all of thirty days—bought a square block in downtown Denver and decreed that the "goldarnedest most beautiful thee-ayter in the world" be built upon it. He sent six architects, including W. J. Edbrooke, who had built the University of Notre Dame in Indiana, all over the world scouting ideas, precious woods, brocade and chandeliers for his milliondollar effort. After sixteen months, the brick and limestone fivestory Tabor Grand was finished.

The main entrance led into a vestibule, the floor of which was laid with old English tiles. Then a marble staircase led up to the rotunda roofed with stained cathedral glass. Next came the foyer, elaborately decorated, which formed a promenade behind the dress circle. Between the entrances of the foyer were panel paintings of wild flowers framed in antique gold and on either side of the entrances were immense mirrors from France. All the woodwork throughout the theater was of cherry imported from Japan, and the massive pillars were heroic in scale. The chair frames in the boxes were solid silver. Seven artists had been brought to Denver to paint an evening sky on the ceiling and golden harps with laurel leaves in the four spandrels. Crowning the proscenium and opening into a semicircular panel was an oil painting of Hector's farewell to Andromache.

In the center of the proscenium the architects originally had installed a huge portrait of Shakespeare.

"Who's that?" Tabor asked.

"Shakespeare," was the reply, "the English writer."

Tabor barked: "What'd he ever do for Denver?" And had it replaced with a portrait of himself.

The curtain itself was a work of art—Tabor had paid the painter Robert Hopkins $15,000 to spend four weeks to depict on the huge cloth a palace at sunset, lofty pillars, broken columns, stairways which led nowhere, and recumbent jungle beasts drowsing amid the ruins.

The opening of the opera house gives a picture of the Denver society of the time—the same type of people who would crowd the courtroom. Here is one account of the greatest social event of the Wild West:

> It was a scene unparalleled in the history of the West. At the moment the doors were thrown open, the audience began to appear. Newly won jewels flashed from ears, necks, and hands of women, many of whom had

been reared in the blight of poverty and had married men no better off than themselves at the start. The yield of the mountains had been kind to them. They seemed like fair flowers lending their loveliness, perfumed air, and jeweled light to Aladdin's garden.

The orchestra commenced the instrumental introduction to "Happy, Happy Day," and the vast drop curtain, which few had noticed in the buzz of excitement, ascended and disclosed the mad scene from "Lucia di Lammermoor." Miss Abbott had chosen this as the best vehicle for her vocal flexibility. The stellar role in "Maritana," a lighter opera, did not provide such opportunities.

At the conclusion of "Lucia," the curtain dropped, the lights went up, and the audience saw a small table in the center of the great stage. The master of ceremonies stepped forward. He called Tabor to the stage. There was to be a speech from the mighty Midas, the giver of this marvelous theater to the city of Denver.

Amid thunderous applause, Tabor stepped forward from the wings. He was attired in evening dress, and a huge diamond flashed from his boiled shirt. He bowed awkwardly to the audience and dropped heavily into a great gilt chair drawn up beside the table. There the mighty one squirmed and fidgeted like a frightened boy who had to go somewhere before he spoke his piece.

It took the master of ceremonies twenty minutes to deliver one of the worst speeches ever heard on such an occasion. He concluded by reading a poem, dedicated to Tabor, which was so bad that Eugene Field, sitting in Box F, had to be restrained by his friends from hurling his mahogany chair onto the stage in the hope of hitting the speaker. Next, the speaker presented to Tabor an album edged with gold and containing the autographs of the artists and artisans who had contributed to the making of his theater. There was still another ordeal. The speaker, bringing forth a fob of solid gold, carefully explained its symbolism.

"I wish to say, ladies and gentlemen, in regard to this, that upon this golden tablet (meaning the fob) is engraved the history of Lieutenant Governor Tabor. This represents an ore bucket. It is filled with nuggets of gold. From the handle of the bucket is suspended a spade, a shovel and a pick, woven into the monogram of Governor Tabor. Then follows the picture of a mule. That mule, let me say, stands in front of a beautiful engraving of the old store where the governor passed so many years. Here are the steps of a golden ladder, *Labor omnia vincet*. Upon this ladder Mr. Tabor began to climb. Next to this is the Tabor Block. Then there is another climb, and at the top is a beautiful engraving of the magnificent edifice in which we are tonight."

The presentation was made amid more applause, and Tabor stuffed the fob into his pocket hurriedly, for he had been called upon to speak. All his swagger seemed to have departed. He appeared to be sorely in need of a friend. Never before had he faced such a discriminating audience.

Baby Doe, sitting in the orchestra circle, a veil covering her pretty face, leaned forward to catch his words.

She knew he was her Santa Claus, and she believed in fables.

One might expect a man as popular as Tabor, with his wealth of political and public experience, to extend himself. Instead, he said:

"Ladies and gentlemen: It is sixteen months since I commenced the building of this opera house. At that time I looked Denver carefully over with its people and here I found a town at the base of the Rocky Mountains—

a city of 30,000 to 40,000 inhabitants, the finest city, I think, of its population on the American continent. I said if Denver is to have an opera house, it should have one worthy of the city.

"Here is the opera house. I shall leave it to your judgment if I have done my duty in this respect. Here is this beautiful album and fob chain—as beautiful as can be. I shall prize them not for their price value, but for the spirit in which they are given."

Amid tumultuous applause, Tabor fled into the wings, the table was removed, and the performance continued. The evening was wearing away and the dramatic critics of the morning newspapers departed in haste to their offices to write the most elaborate and fulsome accounts that perhaps have ever been given to the opening of a theater. The Rocky Mountain *News* became hysterical in its panegyrical appraisement of Tabor's triumph. It swept all other concerns off its front and second pages in the morning and gave its major show windows over to Tabor and the new citadel of the drama, beginning its account in a headline of one word:

PERFECTION!

And not very far from this grand palace of joy was the courthouse where Dr. T. Thatcher Graves would fight for his life in another kind of drama.

Ten

Dramatis personae:

For the prosecution: Isaac Stevens, nicknamed the Pit Bull, district attorney, thirty-three years old, former newspaper editor, politician, tough and smart, with a big future ahead; associate lawyers, James Belford and Lafe Pence, a future congressman. Big team. Very expensive, very clever. Backed by lots of money. Famous. Today it would be like going against a firm called Nizer, Belli and Bugliosi.

For the defense: Second rate. Judge Henry Furman, forty-one, fiery, Texan, intelligent; his partner Thomas Macon, also a judge, conservative, the oldest of the lawyers at sixty-one; and, from the East, Col. Daniel Ballou—a man to watch: a boyhood friend of T. Thatcher Graves and sometime lawyer for Mrs. Barnaby.

The court was presided over by Judge Amos Rising, age sixty-two, former state senator from Colorado and now Supreme Court commissioner. Considered a very good judge.

Here is what happened on the first day of the trial, Tuesday, December 8, with the opening address by the district attorney, according to a Denver newspaper:

> The courtroom was a madhouse. The bailiffs vainly tried
> to control the tide of humanity which surged through
> the main entrances to the chambers, and extra police
> were found necessary to close the doors. Through the
> private door streamed counsel, witnesses, members of
> the bar and dozens of women who desperately sought to

obtain seats in a reserved section, where the daughters of the murdered woman sat next to John Howard Conrad. The district attorney entered upon his arraignment of the accused in calm, measured words, turning from time to time to stab a finger at Dr. Graves, who sat calm and self-possessed. When a lady seated next to him dropped her key rattling upon the floor, he politely reached down and picked it up. Most of the time his tall form was upright in his chair. Occasionally he clasped his hands across his tightly fitting coat and worked his thumbs thoughtfully. Again he placed his elbows upon the arm of his chair, and let his hands hang idly down. When Mr. Stevens was dealing with the statement the accused was said to have made after Mrs. Barnaby's death, Graves leaned forward. There were deep wrinkles across his brow, but there was no pallor, no nervousness. His attitude and bearing were those of a deeply interested spectator, nothing more, as the rhetoric rolled out:

"May it please your honor, and you, gentlemen, who have been selected as jurors in this case, the crime which is the subject of inquiry of the world. It is unique, original, cowardly, dastardly and infamous. It would have struck terror into the heart of the most reckless criminals during the decline of the Roman Empire, when poison was most artfully administered with a splendid daring of indifference. It puts to shame the accomplished efforts of the ancient Egyptians. It has been left for the splendid advancement of civilization for the utilization of the means by which that advance has been made to furnish to the world a more nefarious, a more absolutely reckless crime of murder by poison than any ever before dreamed of. The mails of the national government carry destruction and death. The artery through which flows a great commercial and social life carries insidious and deadly poison

104

Mrs. J. H. (Barnaby) Conrad
The adulterous wife

Isaac N. "Ikey" Stevens
The pugnacious district attorney

along with a billet doux; side by side with the greeting of friends comes the message of death. To ascertain and to punish the perpetrator of this heinous deed is the sole purpose of this investigation!"

District Attorney Stevens rattled on for nearly four hours, outlining the case and painting Graves as a deep-dyed villain who was afraid Mrs. Barnaby was going to dump him as her business manager, and who craved the money he knew he was mentioned for in the will.

He dreaded the ascendency and influence which others might obtain over this old lady, and feared from the reports which he received from Sallie Hanley, the maid, and from others, that he was gradually losing his influence and control over her. He saw in his nightly dreams the vision of this golden egg, the whole of which he had hoped to possess himself, getting farther and farther away. He looked with terror upon the probability of having to rely entirely for support upon the impecunious revenue which his profession had heretofore brought him. This final $80,000 was paid to Dr. Graves as Mrs. Barnaby's agent on the twenty-first day of March, 1891. He immediately, for a reason which needs no explanation, on account of what I have just said, through his brother-in-law, Mr. Roberts, who lived in the city of Boston, acting as broker for him, invested the greater amount of said sum in unregistered bonds and stocks in various electric railroads and other companies, which of course, could at any time be transferred or sold by the doctor himself without the consent of any one, which was done entirely without the knowledge or consent of Mrs. Barnaby.

We will show you, gentlemen of the jury, beyond any doubt in the world, that the defendant on trial was the only person in the world who could have had any possible motive for the destruction of the life of this old woman. We will show you by proof, both direct and circumstantial, that the contents of this bottle, which was mailed in Boston, were prepared by Dr. Graves and by him alone. We think we will be able to show you beyond any question that the inscription on the bottle, *Wish you a happy New Year. Please accept this fine old whiskey from your friend in the woods,* is in the doctor's handwriting.

This is the most remarkable crime of any that was ever committed in the history of the United States, and the whole country will carefully and studiously watch its progress. If it is desired that the interests of the community which you represent shall be protected and that Colorado shall have the reputation of enforcing its criminal laws—and we can prove to you the facts which I have attempted to outline, or enough of them to convince you beyond a reasonable doubt of the defendant's guilt of the crime charged, we will expect you to be courageous, patriotic and law-abiding enough to not allow any appeal to your sympathy, any sophistry or any hair-splitting arguments which may be advanced to save one more defendant to the credit and glory of those who pride themselves upon their ability to acquit the most reckless and daring of criminals, but to return a verdict which can be sustained and applauded and upheld by your fellow men, whatever the verdict may be.

So went the district attorney's blistering opening statement. It seems admirably presented, and things looked bad for Dr. Graves immediately. Yet he listened with dignity, attentively, and shook his head several times with a little smile as though at the absurdity of the charges.

The next morning was Graves' turn, as his lawyer, Judge Furman, far less known than the district attorney, made his presentation for the defense. A Texan given to flowery rhetoric, he was in marked contrast to the cool, comparatively understated Stevens. Judge Furman slapped his thighs as he stalked up and down in front of the jury denouncing the charges and the persecuting motives of John Howard Conrad. He spoke to the jury intensely, looking each in the eye as though addressing only him, interested in only his opinion.

Dr. Graves watched his counsel carefully and confidently, occasionally smiling when Furman became eloquent. When he finished Graves rose and shook his hand.

Furman's address at times reminds me of Jack Finney's comment about the flowery speech of a prosecuting attorney in another nineteenth century murder trial, "a speech that would be better illustrated than presented in words."

On to Judge Furman's address. (I know it is disconcerting to refer to "Judge" Furman, when he is a defense lawyer and the presiding judge is Judge Rising, but that is the way it is recorded.)

Most humbly we do not come before you gentlemen, asking any favor, or with any unreasonable theories, but we come before you with the plain and simple truth. We cannot boast, as has the prosecution, that we have millions of dollars on our side. We rely upon the plain and simple truth. Gentlemen, you have heard the opening statement of the prosecution, and as intelligent, fair-minded and honorable men, who want to hear both sides before you make up your minds, you are now doubtless anxious to hear what the defense has to say upon the statement which has been made against us. Gentlemen, when you have heard that statement, and the testimony by which we will support it, you will see that there are two sides to this case.

If it be true that a bottle of poison was, as the state

107

claims, sent in the manner in which the state claims it was sent, then I go further than the district attorney, who says the man who sent it was a coward. I say the man who sent it is a hell-deserving assassin, and that burning him at the stake would be a mild form of punishment indeed. Gentlemen, in the closing of his remarks the prosecuting attorney asked you to render a verdict that would be sustained by the people of the United States. I ask you, gentlemen, to put that idea out of your minds. I ask you, are you going to pander simply to public feelings? Are you going to pay attention to the cry, as did Pontius Pilate, of "Crucify him, crucify him"? I ask you, gentlemen, to render an honest verdict, let it shake and let it please whom it may.

On Furman rolled in rhetorical turgidity, as he presented Dr. Graves' *bona fides:*

At the age of eighteen Dr. Graves accepted employment with the firm of Rufus Green and Company, and accompanied their manager, Mr. William E. Hyams, to Zanzibar, an island on the eastern coast of Africa, where the company had extensive factories. After being there something like a year and a half, owing to complications caused by the war, Mr. Hyams was compelled to return to the United States, leaving young Graves, then not quite twenty years old, in the exclusive care, control and management of the entire business of that firm, which represented a capital of nearly $500,000. Dr. Graves remained there until 1863. He had two brothers in the Union Army, and as the war progressed his soul caught fire with the inspiration of patriotism that moved his family and countrymen, and so he wrote home to the company that he desired to return, to surrender an easy

108

and lucrative position, and to take his chances in the great drama of war in discharge of what he thought was his duty to his country.

Furman recounted how Graves was recalled to America to enter the war effort. Although Graves was suffering from some tropical malady, he went directly to the front as a young officer to serve with distinction.

His brother was an aide-de-camp of General Wertsell, and young Graves acted as a voluntary aide until February 1864. Upon the recommendation of General Wertsell, under whose eyes he had acted, as a reward for faithful, unselfish patriotism and devoted and courageous service, he was given a captain's commission in the Federal army.

They say this man who sent this bottle was a coward. This defendant has a commission from the United States Government as brevet major for gallantry upon the field of battle, where brave men stood amid the hail and bullets, canister, grape shot and cannon balls. T. Thatcher Graves, the man whom they say is a coward, was the second Federal soldier to enter Fort Harrison in that memorable charge, and his government rewarded him with a commission as brevet major, which he now holds and prizes as life. He was one of the last men mustered out of the Federal service in 1867. What did he do then? He gratified an ambition which he had long cherished. He began the study of medicine. He entered Harvard College, and as his diploma shows, in 1871 he graduated at the head of his class and delivered the valedictory address in behalf of that graduating class. Now, gentlemen, we attach some little importance to this, and we ask you to note it.

Furman let this soak into the jury for two reasons: First as a measure of character: doctors were respected; and second, to emphasize a point that he would later enlarge upon—a Harvard physician would have chosen a more subtle manner of murder than a heavy load of arsenic in a meat extract bottle.

If circumstances are to be used against us, cannot we see circumstances in our favor? In this connection, when we have an opportunity to put witnesses on the stand, we will prove that there are numerous vegetable poisons, which every scientific physician knows of, which will take human life without leaving a trace behind. He was a man of science, thoroughly skilled, and had he desired to compass the death of this unfortunate lady the means were in his hands and power to have done so without leaving any trace behind, or any evidence of the means by which she died.

They say he was impecunious. Gentlemen, we cannot boast of our millions, and I do not know that it is going to help anybody in this trial. My experience and observation is that more men come honestly by poverty than come honestly by riches. Dr. Graves was never a beggar. His practice in Lynn netted him on an average something like $5,000 per annum. That may be a mere bagatelle to men with millions and the counsel who was so dazzled with wealth on account of association with millionaires, but for you, an honest, hard-working jury, you will not say he was a beggar or impecunious when making, as we will show you, about $5,000 a year.

Mrs. Barnaby came to Denver. The District Attorney says Dr. Graves sent her medicine. That is true. She sent him a telegram, the original of which he now has, asking him to send her some nerve medicine and some medicine for rheumatism, sent in the care of E. S. Worrell, giving the address on Arapahoe Street, and that is the reason why the medicine was sent. We will show that for years she had been taking his medicine almost exclusively. They say that this poison in the bottle was sent eleven days after the money was collected. The collection of that money was immaterial, because there was a written contract and a judgment on the court that the money should be paid. She had a vested right in it, although she might have died before its payment, and her heirs would have received their interest in it just exactly as if it had been paid. That cuts no figure in this case one way or the other, because the payment was bound to come under the judgment of the court, and she could will that as well as she could the ready cash after it was collected.

She was with Mrs. Worrell in California. Mrs. Worrell preceded her in Denver, and mark well this statement. Mrs. Worrell knew, before that poison bottle got here, just when Mrs. Barnaby would get to Denver, and she got here before the poison bottle did. Mrs. Worrell shows up, directly the poisoned bottle shows up, and then poor, unfortunate Mrs. Barnaby shows up. They say that there are certain stamps upon that bottle. We do not dispute it. We do not know. They say that that bottle was mailed secretly and by stealth. Well, gentlemen, if they know that they know more than we do about it. They say there are twenty-five cents too much postage on that bottle. We will prove to you that Dr. Graves was almost daily sending out medicine through the mail to his patients, and that therefore he knew exactly how much postage it would be necessary to put on the bottle; so it must have been mailed by someone who did not know.

111

In fact, Graves had been sending medicine to Mrs. Barnaby at the various stopping points of her western trip.

> They say that these stamps were on sale in Providence. We do not know. It is possible Dr. Graves may have bought such stamps, as he was buying stamps by the $5 and $10 at a time to mail his medicines through the country, and maybe he bought such stamps as these. They say there was something like three thousand of those stamps there and that there are two thousand still there. Dr. Graves did not buy all that were sold. We make no denial that there were such stamps sold there. Dr. Graves does not know whether he bought any of that denomination or not. It is possible he did, because he will show and the stamp clerk will show that he was a large patron in the matter of buying stamps.
>
> Gentlemen, in conclusion, I ask you to consult no one, consult nothing except his honor's charge, consult no fact except in evidence, and then, gentlemen, rise in the majesty and dignity of true manhood, exercise true courage. Physical courage is commendable, but there is a higher and nobler courage than that. There is a moral courage which is sublime. I ask you then, gentlemen, to stand to this record, let it please, let it shake whom it may.

The jammed courtroom applauded Furman's two-hour dramatic and seemingly extemporaneous speech and Judge Rising had to admonish the audience.

The next day was totally occupied with philatelic matters. Has a postage stamp ever been such a vital—perhaps crucial—link in a criminal case before or since?

The issue was simply between orange fifteen-cent stamps and blue fifteen-cent stamps. The prosecution was trying to prove that the murderer mailed the lethal bottle from Boston, but since there were no orange fifteen-cent stamps available in Boston at that time as there were in Providence, the murderer possibly or probably came from that city. Circumstantial but damaging, if not actually damning, evidence. Clerk Devenish of the Providence post office testified after the Boston postal clerk had sworn that they had sold no orange Webster fifteen-cent stamps for over a year.

So, it was fairly well established that the murderer might be from Providence, or at least had purchased the stamps there. Unless, of course, the murderer had bought the blue stamps some months previously at some other post office—one of the 9,122 post offices in New England at that time, as John Howard Conrad had said.

But think of the quirk of fate that led Frank Schermerhorn to tear the stamps off the package, to contribute to his son's collection, rather than throwing them out with the rest of the wrapping! That evidence would weigh heavily against Graves in the long run.

Although it seemed obvious what had killed Mrs. Barnaby, the entire next day was taken up with the subject of the actual poison used; Judge Macon tried to raise doubts in the jury's minds in several ways—one feeble explanation was that the woman, though arsenic was found in her body, could have died from pneumonia, her official death certificate before the autopsy having been listed as "congestion of lungs." The prosecution also was out to prove that only a person trained in chemistry like Dr. Graves could have made the solution arsenite of potassium. The defense tried to prove it could have been made from Fowler's Solution, a medicine containing some arsenic available without a prescription at many drugstores and usable for murder by anyone. Conrad had paid for excellent medical men to testify: Professor J. A. Sewall, of Denver University; Professor Walter S. Haines, of Rush Medical College, Chicago, and Professor William P. Headden, formerly of Denver University, but now of the Dakota School of Mines, were the experts for the prosecution. They testified that two grains of arsenic, the basic ingredient of arsenite potassium, is a fatal dose; that the bottle from which Mrs. Barnaby drank contained fifteen or sixteen ounces; and that there were eleven or twelve grains of the poison in each ounce of the liquid. Professor Haines testified that the arsenic used in the preparation of the fatal solution was deadlier and more certain of causing a fatal result than any other variety of the poison.

The bottle out of which Mrs. Barnaby drank was then introduced in evidence. Judge Macon picked it up, held it in front of the spectators and slowly read aloud the words on the label. He pulled out the stopper, placed the mouth of the bottle to his lips, and pretended to take a swig.

"Humph," said the lawyer, smacking his lips, "that wouldn't hurt anyone."

The associate counsel for the defense handled the poison more gingerly. Colonel Ballou sniffed at a couple of ounces poured into a glass. Mr. Furman dipped his fingers into it and tapped the end of his tongue. Then Judge Macon passed the poison to the jury. The twelve men in turn smelled of it, then handed the bottle back. It was passed to Dr. Graves, who examined it for a long moment, tipping the glass, smelling it, then returned it to Judge Macon, remarking with a laugh, "I don't believe that's whiskey."

Mrs. Graves was seen in court for the first time. She came in the morning with her husband and sat by his side all day. A newspaper report described her as a "neat little lady, apparently much younger than her husband, and affects gray colors. Her hat, however, was trimmed with a dove's wing and dark green velvet. She carried a fan, which her husband assisted her in using at times. Her presence had a visible effect in animating the spirits of the accused. He appeared to be very proud of her, and made it his special duty to introduce her to all his acquaintances."

"Mrs. Graves can have a seat right here, by your side," said Judge Macon.

114

"All right," replied the doctor, "but can't you get her a better chair than that?"

He discarded the little chair and got one of the large court chairs for her. Mrs. Graves "acknowledged this courtesy of her husband with a graceful little bow and a smile that captivated the spectators."

The chemists and the autopsy experts went on for another day. Then a day was spent on the arrival of the bottle at the Schermerhorn office; opening it, smelling of the contents, laughing over the inscription—*Happy New Year* in April—and the junior Worrell taking it home. "I wasn't feeling well that day," said Schermerhorn, "and had it been blueberry wine I would have had a glass of it." And the prosecuting attorney said drily, "Had you done that, Mr. Schermerhorn, you would now be fertilizer for blueberries."

Quite a wag, "Ikey" Stevens. And very efficient. He would go far. The daily national publicity he was getting from this case would help him enormously.

Meanwhile, Judge Macon and the defense were doing their best; Considerable time (and tedium for the spectators) was spent on the mechanics of the arrival and delivery of the bottle, to show that it had been opened, handled and was available to several persons for many days before Mrs. Barnaby's arrival; plenty of time and opportunity for someone to empty any real whiskey in the bottle and substitute a deadly arsenical solution.

The opening day of the third week of the trial was an emotion-packed one. When Mrs. Carrier described the touching scene in Mrs. Barnaby's death chamber the emotions of the painful ordeal came back to her with such overmastering force that she broke down completely. She wept freely, and covered her eyes with her handkerchief. There was deep silence in the courtroom, which was broken only by the hysterical sobs of the ladies who had gathered to hear the testimony. Even Judge Rising was visibly affected, and several times wiped the tears from his eyes. Mrs. Graves was moved to a sympathetic degree, and Judge Furman nervously tore

115

at folded paper in temporary embarrassment. The jury "turned away their faces and wiped their moistened eyelids, repressing their emotions. John Howard Conrad wept at the recital of this circumstance of the death of his mother-in-law and, after regaining partial composure, left the courtroom and did not return until the witness had left the stand."

Poor dear fellow; he hadn't seen or communicated with his beloved mother-in-law for four years.

If nothing else, the day helped prove John Howard Conrad a pretty good crier; especially after young Worrell's wife's grandmother concluded her testimony (we know people talked and looked different then, but did they cry easier? For example, did the jury and spectators cry through the Manson case? Or the Patty Hearst case?)

"I was there nearly half of the time during the entire siege of their illness. When Mrs. Barnaby had recovered consciousness, Mr. Worrell, Jr., came into the room where she lay and tenderly touched her hand. When he left tears came into her eyes and she said to me: 'He has been a good boy to me. He has been like my own son, and if it hadn't been for him I would have died before morning.'"

Tears came into the witness' eyes. Her voice choked and "the emblems of grief showed through the elderly witness' glasses." She had to collect herself and then went on. John Howard Conrad, who, during the morning, had "battled hard to control his emotions, broke down with the touching words and spectacle of the silver-haired woman on the witness stand, and he burst into tears."

One unknown but perspicacious reporter wrote chillingly that, while watching Conrad cry, "Mrs. Graves studied him in his grief, with an air of nonchalance, a smile playing over her features, her beautiful black eyes enigmatic and unfathomable."

The elderly witness, opinionated and feisty, rambled on at some length until Stevens got her "back on track."

As we are beginning to see from the agile Mr. Stevens' perfor-

116

mance, he can get just about anybody back on any track he wants; T. Thatcher Graves is going to be child's play for him. The transcript records:

"Tuesday morning Mrs. Barnaby appeared to be feeling better," she continued. "She said she thought, when Mrs. Worrell said it was 'vile stuff' that she didn't like whiskey. When she drank it she said it left a very bad taste in her mouth. Friday morning she was suffering terribly, and it was with great difficulty that she was enabled to breathe. She said she felt very much worse than she ever had before. I had a talk with her then."

"What was said at this conversation?"

"I asked her if she thought the Bennetts could have sent that bottle to her. She replied: 'Oh, no, they would not have done it. I intended to spend next summer with them. I—' She paused and continued faintly: 'Can it be possible that Dr. Graves could do such a thing?' 'I am sure I don't know, Mrs. Barnaby,' I replied."

Eleven

The next two days were filled with uneventful and familiar material, the testimony of Edward Worrell, Jr. and the sixteen-year-old Swedish maid, Nellie Nelson, all corroboration of known events. The only detail of interest to the defense was the fact that the fatal bottle was inadvertently left in the buggy during its trip from Worrell's office to his house. It therefore remained overnight and unobserved in the stables some blocks away where Worrell kept his horses. Macon would put this to good use later.

Edward Worrell, Sr. gave his long testimony the next day; a quiet, subdued and credible witness. He testified that Mrs. Barnaby had told him something about her business affairs and Dr. Graves, whom he described as:

". . . an elegant gentleman, aristrocratic, and she would like for him to manage her property. She said Mr. Anthony had written a letter saying Dr. Graves was very capable. I saw the letter and it was as she represented it. That satisfied me, as a friend of Mrs. Barnaby, that her property was safe in the hands of Dr. Graves. I did not tell her she ought to handle her own property. I did not say anything like that. I did say, if I were in her place I would put my money in a trust company. It might cost her a little more, but would be safer."

He was gently grilled:

"Who is Mr. Anthony?"
"He is a Providence gentleman and a member of the Barnaby

119

company. His letter satisfied me of Dr. Graves' qualifications."

"Then, Mrs. Barnaby asked you, in January 1891, to write to Dr. Graves for her will?"

"Yes. She insisted that I should write."

"But Dr. Graves didn't send the will?"

"No."

"Was she annoyed?"

"Very much annoyed. She wanted the will, for what I did not know. She said she wanted to make some changes. She said she had left $25,000 to Dr. Graves, and that was too much. I told her that a new will would redate all others, and that it was unnecessary that she should have the will, which, she told me, Dr. Graves had. My statement seemed to satisfy her partially, but she was still annoyed."

"When at your house did she express any anxiety or fear as to the proper disposition of her property?"

"She did."

"Did she say in January, at your house, in 1891, 'I must do something to protect my property'?"

"No, sir; but she did say once that 'Dr. Graves will ruin me yet.'"

The next few days were full repetitions and confirmations of what the courtroom already knew—testimony from Nellie, the Worrell's maid, from young Mrs. Worrell and old Mrs. Worrell.

Old Mrs. Worrell's antagonism toward Graves was evident and her testimony damaging, such as:

"In the beginning Mrs. Barnaby said Graves was a perfect gentleman and could do no wrong; after this last January she never said a kind word about him."

"Now hold on here!" expostulated the defense attorney. "You say she was unfriendly to Dr. Graves—yet who wrote these letters to Dr. Graves on her last trip?"

120

He held up four letters. Mrs. Worrell looked at them, flushed and conceded with a sigh:

"Mrs. Barnaby—she dictated them to me."

"And do they not each end with the phrase 'To Mrs. Graves I send ardent love and affection and to you, Dr. Graves, the highest regard.'"

"They do."

"That doesn't sound very unfriendly to me!"

Mrs. Worrell sniffed. "Well, Mrs. Barnaby said he was an excellent doctor but not a very good businessman."

"Hardly a capital offense," said the lawyer archly, "and besides we shall show that he was a perfectly adequate businessman."

Then District Attorney Stevens stood up and dropped a bomb:

"Did Mrs. Barnaby ever show you this letter from Dr. Graves? Written over a year ago?"

"Yes—Josephine was very upset about it—cried about it."

"I shall now read it aloud":

October 7, 1890

Mrs. J. B. Barnaby:

My Dear Friend—The executors, having learned from some one lately returned from Blue Mountain Lake or Glen Falls that you are talking quite seriously of purchasing a house or property under the advice or guidance of Edward Bennett (whom they questioned me very closely about), seemed to be determined to bring up the question of placing you under guardianship to avoid any complications of that nature with your property, now or in the future. I wish to explain what being under a guardian means. You could not sign a paper legally. You could not borrow money, you could have nothing charged more than a six-year-old child. You never could step foot again in the Adirondacks, for you could not even leave town, as you could not raise funds. You would have to live in your old house, for they said so, and they were there.

Now, this is a very serious matter, Mrs. Barnaby, and you must fully understand and appreciate it in every way. Have no talk about the matter which may be used against you. I am ready and anxious to give up the charge of your property the moment you cease to do what I know to be best, and every step which I have taken was laid before the executors at the last meeting, and they not only approved of it all, but thanked me, and also approved of what I have laid out for the future. When you are dissatisfied a guardian will be appointed. Very truly yours,

T. THATCHER GRAVES

Stevens then dismissed Mrs. Worrell and called William Wood, a trustee of the Barnaby estate, who promptly denied that the trustees had suggested a guardianship over Mrs. Barnaby.

"I never heard of any of that Adirondack trouble nor anything about Edward Bennett."

In cross-examination Macon got the witness to admit that he hadn't attended every trustee meeting, that he had heard that Mrs. Barnaby was "somewhat reckless with her money" and that Dr. Graves might have had cause to admonish her about overextending her financial boundaries.

Next, the Adirondack guide Ed Bennett was called, he of the "revolting transaction" in the icehouse. Bennett was a far cry from Cooper's romantic Hawkeye of *The Last of the Mohicans*. Bennett's close-cropped head looked more like barbered fur than hair. His nose was cherried from weather and whiskey. Normally in the Adirondacks he thought nothing of wearing the same smoky work-clothes for a week at a time; as someone said, his clothes "were put on him once and for all, like the bark of a tree." But now he wore a fresh city suit, starched shirt, and a tie which he tugged at occasionally as if it were a leash; the clothes, not surprisingly, had

122

come from the Barnaby store in Providence, courtesy of John Howard Conrad—clothes that gave him an uncharacteristic and not wholly convincing air of respectability which he nevertheless seemed to revel in. Rough, tough, loud, expansive—Bennett provided some needed comic relief to the trial:

"Will you please describe to the jury the surrounding country where you live," the district attorney began.

This opened up a floodgate of ersatz Emersonian praise.

Bennett beamed. The yellow teeth of a beaver grinned from chapped lips. "Ah, good gentlemen of the jury! The mountains around my one-hundred-room resort and celestial lakeside place— if you could see them of a twilight, violet at first, then turning into an incredible azure such as..."

"Oh, never mind that!" interrupted Stevens. "Just get on with the facts!"

Everyone laughed.

Reluctantly he gave up the birch bark tourist spiel and returned to Mrs. Barnaby, whom he said he'd known as a guest at the resort for nine years. Nothing was said about an icehouse or "transactions" of any nature.

Later, later. Graves himself would soon be on the stand. But for now it was the voluble Mr. Bennett, putting the doctor and Sallie Hanley down and making himself out to be a capital fellow and worth every cent of the $10,000 Mrs. Barnaby had left him in her will "for his extreme and many—uh—kindnesses over the years."

Bennett rambled on about bucolic, innocent outings:

The witness told of the trip the party had taken up and across the lake. He and Mrs. Barnaby were in one boat.

Mrs. Barnaby bought a bottle of brandy from his brother for three dollars, which Mrs. Graves thought was an enormous price. After the conversation with Graves, already recounted, they stayed all night at Long Lake, then continued their trip. They saw a fawn.

Immediately Dr. and Mrs. Graves thought it would be a great idea to catch it. Mrs. Cleveland was stopping near there, and Dr. Graves thought it would be nice to present it to her.

"Mrs. Cleveland? The wife of President Grover Cleveland?" said Mr. Stevens.

"Ex-President," said someone in the audience.

"Ex-President and next President!" shouted Mr. Furman.

Glances all around. Then the witness went on to tell of the presentation of the fawn to Mrs. Cleveland. "She was delighted, and petted it, but I don't know if Grover wanted it or not," he said with an air as though he and Grover were old chums. Laughter in the courtroom. Bennett was enjoying the captive audience.

The next witness, Mrs. E. S. Bennett, wife of the preceding witness, remembered the visit of Mrs. Barnaby to the Adirondacks, as well as that of Dr. and Mrs. Graves. She had a mouth like a staple, and eyes that seemed to warn: "Scrape those boots before entering."

"Did Mrs. Barnaby ever complain of Dr. Graves?"

"She complained of Sallie Hanley and also of the doctor. When Mrs. Barnaby received the letter threatening guardianship she cried for days. The complaints against Sallie Hanley were that she rode astride a horse 'like a man.' And, then, Miss Hanley fell off a horse and did not tell Mrs. Barnaby. I advised the maid to go and report at once that she fell off the horse, as the deceased would find out about it anyhow, but Miss Hanley did not do so. Mrs. Barnaby was very much displeased at her maid."

The next witness was Mrs. Mary Hickey, the very Irish former housekeeper of Mrs. Barnaby, more friend than servant, and with a brogue that almost needed a translator.

Q. How long did you know her prior to her death?
A. Who?
Q. Mrs. Barnaby. We are speaking of Mrs. Josephine Barnaby.

A. Ah—her.

Q. Yes.

A. I knew her since I been in the United States.

Q. How long is that?

A. Nearly twenty years; first family I ever worked for.

Q. And Dr. Graves?

A. The doctor? Oh well, he came to my house one morning, might be seven, eight o'clock in the morning; I never seen him before; he didn't tell me he was no doctor. He was looking for somebody to do a little work for his wife. And we get to talking and he says, "Mary, don't be at all surprised," he says, "to hear any time that Mrs. Barnaby will have a stroke." I says, "How come you to know that when she looks so healthy and strong!" He says, "She walked uphill to my house"—it is a very steep hill—and he says, "when she got to my house there was purple marks around her eyes."

Q. He was referring to the trip in December when she was there?

A. And he says, "Mary, wait and see." Shook hands with me and I asked him how Mrs. Graves was. He says she is very well, and I said there is nothing I would not do for Mrs. Graves. He says, "Mary, she is a lady, she was born so," and I never seen Dr. Graves afterwards until I seen him in this court.

Mrs. Hickey glanced quickly in the direction of Dr. and Mrs. Graves. The prosecution launched into a tighter re-examination.

Q. Do you know whether or not there was any secrecy about Mrs. Barnaby visiting Dr. Graves' office directly after she got acquainted with him?

A. Well, she didn't like—I don't know the motive she had for it, she came to the door one day, Mrs. Smith was going down the other side of the street, her sister-in-law, and she didn't want Hattie

125

to see her going to Dr. Graves'; at his first acquaintance she didn't care to be seen going there, but after that I suppose she didn't care whether she was seen or not.

Secrecy? Perhaps the tantalizing secrecy that only lovers know, no matter what the age?

The next day would be a devastating one for Graves.

Twelve

The announcement of Henry G. Trickey of the Boston *Globe*, the next witness, sent the courtroom into a tizzy; everyone had read his so-called factual interview with the doctor in Providence; it was on the front page of virtually every newspaper in the country.

A year and a half later he would be angrily condemned by the judge in the Lizzie Borden case as "spurious," castigated and reprimanded for "gross lies" in the press.

According to the *American Heritage Dictionary*, spurious means:

> lacking authenticity or validity, counterfeit; false, illegitimate, bastard.

Mr. Trickey would appear to be all of the above some eighteen months later at the Borden trial, but right now he was riding high with the most sensational interview with the presumed murderer of Mrs. Barnaby that any newspaperman had obtained. While Trickey testified on the stand, Graves was described as "angry, manifestly contemptuous, fists clenched in indignation, and consulted frequently with his attorney."

Henry G. Trickey, his forehead sweaty and twitching, testified for an hour, substantially repeating information that is covered in Chapter Five. Perhaps he was honing his fine talent for lack of veracity that would bloom later at the Lizzie Borden trial.

After he left the stand, Charles E. Lincoln, the Providence correspondent of the Boston *Herald*, was called and testified:

"I have known Dr. Graves by sight four years. I interviewed him April 27 last, in the office of the Western Union in Providence. I was there, having just come from the theater. I was talking at the time with E. M. Frentz. The talk I had with the accused began with a statement by Dr. Graves that he thought he was in a position to use a horsewhip on some one of us, and that he would do so if he could find the proper one. He was asked why. He replied that someone had sent a decoy message to his wife, asking her to meet him at Danielsonville. Dr. Graves wrote a message to his wife then, telling her to come back to Providence.

"I had a conversation with the doctor about the deceased. He said he was appointed her business agent on her own solicitation, which was repeated three times. He said Mrs. Barnaby had many lovers, and that he had been requested by her daughters to keep many things secret. He told me of the Bennett muss, and said Bennett was a loafer and a drunkard. He told me an autopsy had been held, and that Mrs. Barnaby had been killed by poison. He said the Denver authorities were making a complete investigation. He said that night that he had not heard of the poisoning of Mrs. Barnaby till he was told by Mrs. Worrell. He said Mrs. Worrell was a coarse woman, and had not been so sick as she pretended. This conversation was held at 11:25 o'clock at night.

"I was the reporter who was the companion of reporter Trickey when the latter interviewed Dr. Graves at his residence, April 28. We went to his house at 7:25. We were admitted at the rear door, and went on the floor to the right. In about five minutes Dr. Graves entered. We talked about extraneous subjects before approaching the Barnaby matter. He said he became acquainted with

128

Hon. Henry Furman
The doctor's counsel

E. S. Worrell, Sr.
A credible witness

the deceased by treating her for paralysis. She was in a low condition, and he gave her much extra attention."

"Who asked the questions of Dr. Graves?"

"Both of us asked questions. He told us he and his wife had been guests of Mrs. Barnaby in the Adirondacks the previous summer. After they arrived he said Mr. Bennett and Mrs. Barnaby drank a good deal, and, looking through a crack in an *old ice house he saw the two lying drunk on the floor with all the indications of a previous revolting transaction.*

"Mr. Trickey then said Mrs. Barnaby must have been a whore. Graves said she was a damned whore in her instincts."

The trial transcript reads w---- and d--- w----, but when Lincoln spoke the vile words, the courtroom buzzed with shocked and titillated voices.

The next witness was the Pinkerton man, Hanscom. Under the district attorney's guidance, he told of the several evenings that he had spent in the Barnaby mansion masquerading as Charles Conrad, while he and John Howard tried to trick or cajole Dr. Graves into confessing. Hanscom's testimony was essentially the same as Graves' initial account. After Hanscom Conrad took the stand and Furman questioned him. He backed up Hanscom's account of the interviews in the mansion. One exchange was interesting.

Q. "Then you never had any quarreling with Dr. Graves those evenings?" asked Furman.

A. "Not the slightest," replied Conrad.

Q. "That is not what your friend, your spy, your employee, your 'brother' Mr. Hanscom said! Why don't you two get together on your lying story about your attempt at a frameup!"

Conrad's jaw jutted and he half rose from his chair. "Don't

129

you dare talk to me like that! You whippersnapper!"

Judge Rising rapped his gavel. "Gentlemen! Get back to the testimony."

Mr. Furman calmed down.

A startling statement occurred during Judge Macon's cross-examination of Conrad. The subject was on another topic but suddenly Conrad stood up in the witness box, stabbed his finger at Colonel Ballou several times and snarled: "And there, gentlemen, is your coconspirator in the plunder of the estate and your co-plotter in the murder!"

Stricken, Macon turned to the judge, his arms spread in a frantic appeal. "Your honor!"

Judge Rising rapped twice with his gavel. "Mr. Conrad, only Dr. Graves is on trial here—you cannot make irresponsible statements like that!"

Conrad: "Even if it's true?"

Judge Rising: "Be quiet, sir!"

Conrad growled, "In Montana trials we aim to get at the truth!"

"Sir, be quiet or you'll be held in contempt and will be going back to Montana sooner than you expect!"

The audience was visibly aroused by this, and not necessarily *against* Conrad's boast of frontier justice. After all, both Colorado and Montana had found vigilante justice a rather neat system, even if a few innocent necks were broken in the process.

Ballou wrote on a notepad and slid it over to Furman.

We shall sue that bastard for $100,000.

Eventually Conrad was quieted and the trial got back on course.

The handwriting experts coincided in the opinion that the comparison of the handwriting on the poisoned bottle with letters written by the defendant to Mrs. Barnaby, and an anonymous threatening letter addressed to Mr. Conrad at Hotel Albany, on December 4, 1891, showed that they were written by the same person. The experts, hired of course by Conrad, were subjected to a grueling cross-examination by the senior counsel for the defense.

Conrad's cross-examination by Judge Macon occupied the forenoon session; he made a vigorous, if overly rehearsed, witness.

"So you and Doctor Graves got along just fine those evenings at the Barnaby mansion, eh?"

"I would say so."

"Then there was never any altercation whatever?"

"There never was and I never revealed what my real feelings were till the night I cried, and then I made no strictures upon him and controlled myself, so he did not suspect what I was aiming at."

"Ah, you wept. You weep a lot?"

"Only when moved or angered."

"What did you weep about this night?"

"He had threatened to heap scandal up about the Barnaby family. I was weeping at the accusations brought by him and his 'dear friend,' Colonel Ballou, in the past against an innocent family." (Perhaps Conrad was afraid that his wife's infidelities, which he was to charge her with having taken place starting in September 1888, would be brought out and wreck his political aspirations.)

"What had Colonel Ballou said?"

"He stated in court when the will contest was up that he would cause a scandal in the Barnaby family unless the suit was settled."

"How do you know he made those remarks?"

"It was published in the Providence papers, and Colonel Winship told me he made the threats of scandal."

"Don't you control both the Providence papers *and* Colonel Winship?"

"Objection!"

"Sustained."

"Was that Winship the same man whom reporter Trickey interviewed on the funeral train between Jersey City and Providence?"

"I didn't hear reporter Trickey's interview. I left the room when he was called because I could not bear to hear the scandalous statements Dr. Graves made to him about Mrs. Barnaby."

"They were not true, then?"

"They were absolutely and maliciously false. Mrs. Barnaby was the best woman that ever lived. Hers was a happy family till she got under the influence of these two men—Dr. Graves and Colonel Ballou. There was never an unkind word spoken in the household."

The witness showed deep feeling, dabbing at his eyes, and it looked for a moment as if he would give way to his emotions. Again.

"There never was an unkind word, you say?"

"There never was, sir. Never was one spoken in my presence, and I was there for fully nine years."

"Do you mean to say that there was never any unkind feeling between Mrs. Barnaby and her daughters?"

"There was never anything but the most cordial feeling between Mrs. Barnaby and her daughters."

(Lies! And why did he never make an effort to see his own son, my father, after the imminent, ugly divorce—for over thirty years— until he was destitute and needed money? This son he would weep over on the witness stand and would "sic on" to this murder case of his "beloved mother-in-law" whom he detested.)

"Will you swear . . . ?"

"I am swearing now!"

"Will you swear it is not true that there was hard feeling between the deceased and her daughters and that they never associated with her?"

"Such a statement is absolutely false."

Macon (quietly, to get attention): "How then, sir, do you explain

132

your mother-in-law's not having seen or written to your wife for forty-eight months before she died?"

"Mrs. Barnaby never wrote a letter. She was a paralytic and could not. Her maid wrote for her."

"Oh, well why is it that she didn't have a letter written to your wife for forty-eight months before her death?"

Objection! Sustained.

"Did you offer Dr. Graves thirty-five thousand dollars if he would admit he sent the bottle to Mrs. Barnaby?"

"No, sir."

"Did you offer any money? Twenty-five thousand dollars?"

"No, sir."

"Is it true that you bore all the expenses of the witnesses for the state?"

"It is true."

"How much would that be?"

"I haven't tallied yet."

"About seventy-five thousand dollars?"

A gasp from the audience—even an audience used to quick riches.

"I haven't tallied yet."

"Did you secure the attendance of Messrs. Lincoln, Trickey and Day?"

"Mr. Day came here of his own volition and instance. I secured the attendance of Messrs. Trickey and Lincoln."

Very sarcastic and slowly: "You...secured...their attendance?"

"Yes."

"You mean...you agreed to pay their expenses?"

"I agreed to do it, and did it."

"Did you also agree to pay them for time they spent?"

"I did."

"How much?"

"No amount was agreed on. I promised them that they should not lose anything by coming," declared Conrad, rather proud of his generosity and of the deepness of his pockets—and indeed they must have been very deep to have kept several dozen witnesses in hotels, food, and "unemployment" for the duration of the six-week trial.

It is not difficult to imagine what passed through Dr. Graves' mind as Conrad gave his odious testimony.

James L. Lindsey was then called by the state.

"I live in Denver. Have been here for eleven years. Have been teller for the First National Bank of Denver, and for the last three years teller for the First National Bank of Aspen. My duties require me to be an expert in handwritings. I am constantly called upon to make examination of signatures."

"You have compared the writing upon this bottle and these letters of Dr. Graves?"

"Yes, sir, and I made memoranda of some of the comparisons. I made these comparisons at Pinkerton's office and here in the courtroom."

"I ask you, Mr. Lindsey, if in your opinion you believe the inscription upon the bottle was written by the same person who wrote these letters?"

"I do."

"Did you not pick out some particular word or letters and compare them with the same letters on the bottle?"

"Yes, sir."

"Now, Mr. Lindsey, will you show me in any one of those letters anything which compared with the writing on the bottle."

In the letter of April 27, Lindsey showed the word "accept" on both the letter and on the bottle, and the two compared closely enough to make it definite in the mind of the witness that the same hand had written both. Another similarity was in the capital letter N as "it occurs in New York and New Year."

134

"You find in the word 'accept' only a similarity between the letters 'pt'?"

"Yes, sir, that's all."

"You say the writing on the bottle was rather better than that in Dr. Graves' letter."

"Yes, sir."

The letters and the bottle were handed to the jury.

In the afternoon James Lindsey continued on the stand.

"This morning you called attention to the letters 'pt,'" said Macon to the witness, "in the letter of April 27. Please indicate the letters used on the letter for comparison."

The witness pointed them out. In a letter of January 1, 1890, the word "New Year" was found. It was believed to correspond to the "New" in "New Years" on the bottle. In the letter from the doctor dated November 10 the word "New" in line ten on the third page possessed a striking resemblance to the inscription. The letter of October 12, page three, had a capital N that looked like the inscription. In the same epistle the letters "f" and "p" on page three were similar to the ones used on the bottle.

The defense lawyer asked, "Does a man write the same way at any two times?"

"Not to a hair."

"Is it common to find a handwriting like Dr. Graves'?"

"It is not."

"Is it so uncommon you never saw another like it?"

"No."

"Did you not know when you made the examination that Dr. Graves was accused of the crime?"

"Yes."

"Were you not asked to pick out the resemblances?"

"I was."

"Were you not asked to pick out all the resemblances?"

"Oh, no."

"When you are given handwriting to compare, do you make first a general comparison from an inspection of all the letters in the document, or do you pick out particular resemblances?"

"Oh, a general comparison."

"Now, when you read these letters, didn't you find more letters that did not than that did correspond to the inscription?"

"I think not."

Macon bore in hard. Lindsey was a tough witness, sure of himself.

"Do not men, writing under different circumstances, make their letters so differently that no expert can identify them?"

"I shouldn't say so."

"Have you not found that letters in the same words, written by the same hand, are as often dissimilar as alike?"

"I should say not."

"Is it not true that signatures are more likely to be identical at different times than ordinary writing?"

"Yes."

"Were you ever called upon to detect cases of attempt to disguise writing?"

"Once, before the Free Masons. I gave my opinion. What their decision was I know not," Lindsey replied primly.

"Is there any evidence in the writing of the inscription of an attempt to conceal?"

"I think so."

"In what letter?"

"In the letter 'e,' which is made like a capital."

"If you had not been told Dr. Graves was guilty would you ever have dreamed that the writing was a disguise?"

The witness did not understand the question.

"Why do you think there is evidence of the attempt to conceal in the inscription?"

"Because it is unlike the writing in the letters."

136

"Oh! And you reasoned for the principle that one had written both!" exclaimed Macon exultantly.

The witness admitted that he did.

"As a banker was not one of your duties to detect counterfeit bills?"

"Yes."

"How do you tell that a bill is counterfeit?"

"I can't state."

"Is it intuition?"

"No, but your question is like asking one to explain a general opinion."

"Don't you examine the signature on the bill?"

"Oh, no."

"What do you examine?"

"The entire bill."

"And the signature, too?"

"No, you couldn't tell a bill was counterfeit by examining a signature."

"Suppose two bills were given to you and you had never seen the President's signature, how would you tell which was counterfeit, or whether either was?"

The witness made an attempt to explain, and Macon asked:

"Is it not true that there are no evidences of an attempt to conceal in handwriting, standing alone?"

"Sir, if you were to give me the bottle and nothing else, I could not know there was an attempt to conceal. I did use the letters of the accused as a basis of comparison."

"Then, if there is an attempt to conceal, the best experts could not detect it?" Macon suggested.

"According to my idea, they could not."

The state recalled the witness, and he said he believed Dr. Graves wrote both the inscription and the letters. Suddenly Kitty Graves stood up in court and said in a loud voice, "Dr. Graves did

137

not write that label!" Then she fell back in her chair and seemed to be in a faint. She was helped from the court, the room buzzed and Dr. Graves looked distraught. But the judge pounded his gavel and the trial went on.

Leo Capallier was then called to the stand. His calm voice was lightly laced with an accent.

"Born in Calais, France. Have lived in this country for about eighteen years. I have made a special study of handwriting for about nine years. Had six years experience in this line of work before coming to Denver. I have examined the writing on this bottle and also that of the letters of Dr. Graves. The first thing I noticed was the small letter 'a.' The same formation was used in this letter both on the bottle and in the letters. In starting the letter 'a' there is a tendency to start the letter with a curve, which is especially marked at the top."

On being cross-examined by Macon the witness admitted that he taught French for a living.

"You...teach..." savoring every word..."French...for...a living?"

"Yes, sir."

Then pouncing: "Not handwriting?"

"No, sir."

"Not the science of handwriting?"

"No, sir."

Macon looked significantly at the jury, then snapped: "Who paid you to come here, and how much?"

Objection!

Sustained.

Macon then led the witness through a long questioning in regard to the formation of letters. "Did you notice whether or not in his letters Dr. Graves always crossed his 't's?"

The witness, showing off, and off the point, replied pedantically: "People who cross their 't's' above the stem are dreamers, idealists. People who cross their 't's' at mid-stem are inclined to be practical."

Macon, irritated: "Fascinating! Now let's get back to the point. We don't care where and how Dr. Graves crossed his 't's'—only if he crossed them at all. Now pay attention, sir! In all those letters did Dr. Graves cross his 't's'?"

"I can't say."

"Well, let me put it another way. Was there one instance that you noticed where he did *not* cross his 't'?"

"No, sir."

Holding up the bottle: "Do you observe that in this inscription only one 't' is crossed?"

"Yes, sir."

"Ah, clever of you!" Macon said decisively.

Next, an important witness.

Daniel R. Ballou, Esq., of Providence, a corpulent gentleman with a diamond stickpin, side chops, a great moustache and a wide-eyed expression. He was described as "looking like a walrus observed on the Galápagos Isles after having just sat upon a very sharp rock." Ballou stated that he was a lawyer, had practiced law for twenty-six years, and from 1867 until 1875 was Clerk of the Court of Common Pleas in the city of Providence. He was not going to have an easy time of it. Macon is doing the tough questioning:

Q. You know Dr. Graves, of course?

A. I first knew Dr. Graves about thirty-five years ago, while a student in Ross Institute at Thompson, Connecticut, and some four years ago, he appeared in my office one day and renewed the acquaintance, saying he was very glad to see me, and had supposed until within a very short time previous that I had been killed in the service.

(A good old boy chuckle) Said he was glad the rumor was false."

Though not stated explicitly, not yet anyway, Ballou is also on trial here for collusion in fraud—and complicity in murder. Though this is the defense lawyer, he is trying to anticipate the prosecution's implications that Graves got Ballou into the act to be her attorney, break the will, get Graves mentioned in the new will, and then they would murder her.

Q. When did you become acquainted with Mrs. Barnaby?

A. Some time early in the month of October, 1889.

Q. Did she disclose what business she wanted done at that time?

A. She wanted an attorney to contest the will.

Q. You say some days before that petition was to be heard, Mr. Tillinghast came to your office as the representative of the estate?

A. Yes, sir?

Q. What was his mission there, from what he said?

A. To suggest a compromise.

Q. Now, you may state whether there was at that time any compromise reached, provisionally, between you and Mr. Tillinghast.

A. Nothing, not at that time; it was a mutual agreement for a cessation of hostilities and continuance of the application for an allowance.

Q. What statement, if any, did you ever make, or what purpose, if any, did you ever have if this litigation proceeded hostilely, to make any attack upon Mrs. Barnaby's character?

Objection.

Q. Mr. Conrad swore expressly that is what Mr. Ballou stated he would do, may it please the court.

Though Rising was considered a fair judge previous to this trial, notice how seldom the defense wins a point. The district attorney is in Conrad's pocket; could the judge be also?

Judge Rising: I don't think it is competent; it is not evidence that this man can tell what his purpose was.

Q. Let that pass. State whether you ever uttered an expression during the pendency of this will difficulty which contained a threat

140

that you would attack Mrs. Barnaby's character if this litigation proceeded hostilely?

A. No, sir.

Judge Belford: I object to that question.

Macon: Mr. Conrad swore that he threatened to make an attack upon Mrs. Barnaby's character. My question was, "Did you ever?" I ask you, Colonel Ballou, whether at one place or another, did you ever make any such threat?

A. I never did.

Q. Mrs. Barnaby was your client?

A. She was my client.

Q. Did anybody make such a threat to you, interested in this business?

A. I can't say there was directly any such threat made, but inferentially there was.

Q. What were the words?

Objected to as immaterial.

The court: He answered your question, Judge Macon.

Q. Who was it: somebody representing the estate?

A. The attorney of the estate, Mr. Tillinghast.

Q. Give the words that he used.

Mr. Pence: I object, as incompetent and immaterial; Mr. Tillinghast in no wise appears in this controversy.

Macon: One-half of this testimony has been directed to showing that Colonel Ballou and Dr. Graves robbed this woman, and in doing so they have sworn that Colonel Ballou, as well as Dr. Graves, had spoken of Mrs. Barnaby in the most disrespectful terms. Now, we have a right to show that no such conspiracy ever existed, that no such language was ever used by him, and whatever slander to Mrs. Barnaby came from the other side!

The court: Part of that is correct and part not. You haven't a right to show that some person not a party to this prosecution ever made any such statements. That doesn't disprove it at all.

Q. Mr. Ballou, at that interview with Mr. Tillinghast, did you come to any conclusion?

A. No, sir, except for a cessation of hostilities by a continuance of the petition for allowance which I was informed they proposed to contest.

Q. Tell the jury what the results of these preliminary negotiations were.

A. I was asked on what terms I would settle, or Mrs. Barnaby would settle her claims upon the estate. I told the attorney, Mr. Tillinghast, we would settle for one hundred and fifty thousand dollars, and release all claims to the estate. Mr. Tillinghast said that that would not be possible...

Objection!

Q. Just give the result.

A. The result was that after a discussion we arrived at a sum of one hundred and five thousand dollars.

Q. Before you finally accepted this offer whom did you consult?

A. I laid the matter before Dr. Graves as the friend of Mrs. Barnaby. I then went to Pawtucket and consulted with the Honorable Robert Sherman, a relative of Mrs. Barnaby, and laid the whole matter before him, and invited his advice as to the advisability of accepting the compromise offer.

Q. Who else did you consult?

A. Mrs. Barnaby, that was all.

Q. What did you retain for your fee?

A. I retained ten thousand dollars. Mrs. Barnaby asked me before the compromise agreement was formulated what my charge would be for my services in the case covering the whole service. I told her I thought I ought to have ten thousand dollars. The responsibility was large, and the amount was large; and she remarked she thought that the fee was a little large. I told her that I didn't feel that way about it, and she acquiesced at once in the reasonableness of the bill.

Was Colonel Ballou sweating a little? Even though he sounded so smooth, so plausible? The drilling continues:

Q. State to the jury as briefly as you can, and as fully as the facts justify, your connection with the drawing of the will, which we call the Providence will, for Mrs. Barnaby, and when you first were required by her, or requested, to draw her will.

A. I was first requested to draw her will a very few days after the twelfth of November, the day upon which the final agreement of compromise was signed. Mrs. Barnaby came into the office alone on that occasion, and said that she would like for me to draw her will. I said to her, "I don't think, Mrs. Barnaby, I would be in a hurry about drawing my will just yet." She replied that she wanted to go to Saratoga and desired to have the will drawn before she went away. "Well," I said, "we will talk it over," and we did talk it over, and she produced a memorandum upon which was given the way she wanted her will drawn, that is mentioning the legatees and the amount, and the disposition of her real estate which she had inherited from her father. I went through each item very carefully with her, as is invariably my custom in drawing wills, and many changes were made at her suggestion, and after we had gone through it and she had fully explained what she desired and how she wanted it, she wanted to know if it could appear in the will or if I could state in any way in the will the reason why she did not give anything to her daughters. I said yes.

At this prosecuting attorney Lafe Pence rose apprehensively: I object! It is immaterial and not pertinent!

Macon, with some sarcasm: It has been testified by several witnesses that the marvelous relations between Mrs. Barnaby and her daughters were as affectionate as are usually found to be between mother and daughter. Now, I want to show that the relations were— (he looked around the courtroom casually, then whirled and shouted) —were ROTTEN! And that they were estranged—hadn't seen each other or written for years!

Loud objections.

The court: I don't think it is at all material.

Macon: Oh well, just let it pass. (To the witness): Was there any part of that will drawn contrary to Mrs. Barnaby's desires?

A. No, sir.

Q. And was it drawn so as to the phraseology suited her?

A. Yes. She remarked that it was just the way she wanted it.

Q. What did you do with the will after it was drawn and she had signed and the witness had signed?

A. I put it in an envelope and sealed it up and directed it, "The last will and testament of Josephine A. Barnaby, to be delivered to Dr. T. Thatcher Graves upon my decease."

Q. Where was Dr. Graves, if you know, when you were drawing that will, or when Mrs. Barnaby presented the memorandum to you in the first place?

A. I don't know anything about that; I had no consultation with Dr. Graves or didn't see him or pass a word with him during the whole transaction.

Q. So he did not see the will.

A. Why should he have?

Q. And you didn't tell him its contents?

A. Of course not! Totally unprofessional.

Q. From the first time you ever had any relations with her in a business way until the last time you saw her, and in all of the interviews, what was her condition of mind?

A. Mrs. Barnaby, barring her infirmity, which caused a halting of speech and halting of thought, was a very bright person and an attractive older woman.

For the first time we get a first-hand, believable description of the victim.

It took her some time to express herself, but, giving her time and having a little patience with her, she was very clear and cogent

144

in all her thought and expression; I think wonderfully so for one laboring under her infirmities.

There was talk about a letter from Mrs. Barnaby which Ballou turned over to Graves' lawyers in Denver. Stevens went on the attack:

Q. Speaking of professional, did you yourself, colonel [who was shocked at the breach of etiquette] regard it as *professional* to give to Dr. Graves, who had paid you no fee, the secrets of Mrs. Barnaby, who had paid you ten thousand dollars for your services?

A. I think when a man's life is at stake a person...

Q. Answer the question!

A. I did not in this case consider it unprofessional! I also want to correct one piece of testimony which I have given. At the time I was asked the question it slipped my mind. You had asked me the question if I paid anything out of this ten thousand dollars or made any present out of it and I answered you that I did not.

Q. Yes, sir.

A. I did, afterwards. Mr. Jackson and I gave Dr. Graves a check for five hundred dollars, a finder's fee, in consideration of the fact that he had suggested Mrs. Barnaby's coming to us. I want you to have it all.

Q. Ooh—that slipped your mind entirely a while ago, did it? That little matter?

A. Yes, sir.

Q. What refreshed your recollection, please?

A. Upon reflection it occurred to me that I had.

Q. Have you been thinking and considering whether it would be better to own up, or to get caught at it afterwards?

A. No, sir.

Q. It had entirely escaped your mind?

A. It did, for the moment.

Q. *Moment?* More than an hour has passed since then. Why did you not correct it earlier?

A. Because it had no connection with what we've been talking about since.

Q. Did you *think* of it at that time? Just a fleeting thought, say?

A. It didn't occur to me at that time; this occurred, I should say, directly after this transaction was closed.

Q. When you got the ten thousand dollars what did you do with it, deposit it in the bank?

A. We deposited this check, and I gave a check to Mr. Jackson, my partner, for $4,750, and I took one myself, but whether the five hundred dollar check to Dr. Graves was made at that time or the next day I would not undertake to say.

Q. Is it your habit in your office to divide every night what you make?

A. No, just every time we get a large fee—we never had as large a fee as that before.

Q. Never had occasion to divide a ten thousand dollar swag before, had you, colonel?

A. *Swag*, sir?

Q. (Snarling) Booty—money—pelf!

A. No, sir.

From the transcript it is not hard to visualize the combatants. Defense laywer, rising: "May I respectfully ask the court to admonish the learned counsel to kindly curb his nasty tone of voice and generally vitriolic attitude to all the witnesses?

Judge Rising: "So observed."

Stevens, hands folded, Uriah Heep fashion, bent mock humbly: "Gentle sir, might one pry into your private affairs enough to perhaps ascertain whether or not you and Jackson never received as large a fee as that before?"

Laughter in the courtroom.

The witness resumed:

A. No, sir, that is the largest fee we ever received.

146

Edward Bennett
A real "friend in the woods"

Col. Daniel R. Ballou
Graves' dubious partner

Q. You say that you gave Mrs. Barnaby more than the usual explanation of the contents of the will?

A. Yes.

Q. Why did you do that, pray tell?

A. Because she said to me that the relations of her family towards her weren't pleasant, and I thought it was a cautionary measure I ought to take to see that this will was properly made in every respect.

Stevens abruptly realizes he has opened a can of worms that he doesn't want to get into and switches topics.

Q. The memorandums she originally brought you contained a mention of Dr. Graves, did it, for twenty-five thousand dollars?

A. I think it did.

Q. Oh, come on now—you *know* damn well it did!

A. Yes, I know it did.

Q. I want to know what "family secrets" you have ever disclosed to anybody.

A. I never have divulged any secrets, as I understand secrets. I didn't desire to make this statement with reference to any scandal.

Q. What fee do you get in this case?

Objection.

Objection overruled.

Q. Mr. Tallman came to me in May and wanted to know if I would...

Q. Answer the question! How much are you to get?

A. There has been no fee fixed, except the retainer I was paid; I am to be paid what the services are reasonably worth; the retainer was one thousand dollars.

Q. How much is the balance to be?

A. There is no agreement whatever, according to the services I render.

Q. What do you expect?

A. I haven't expected.

Q. Isn't it contingent on the result of the case in any way?

A. No, sir, perhaps you do, but I don't make such kind of fees.

Q. You say the doctor was surprised when you gave him the five hundred dollars?

A. I think he was.

Q. Entered a huge protest against it, I suppose?

A. I think he said, "What is this for?"

Q. Oh, come now—didn't he say, "Where the hell is the other forty-five hundred dollars?"

A. No, sir, he damn well did not!

Judge Rising: Language, sirs, language!

When would the *sine qua non* of this trial, Dr. Graves, testify? Soon, very soon, only a day away.

But first: T. J. Dalzell was to be called next. We remember him as the old friend Graves spent the day with in Denver while waiting for Mrs. Barnaby's remains to be transported east, the man to whom Graves had confessed his dalliance with a married woman he met on the train, and hence missed trains and arrived thirty-six hours overdue in Denver.

Before taking the stand, Dalzell, a compact, well-dressed, boyish-looking business man who was very well thought of in Denver, passed a note to Graves.

"Tom!—It's important for your case—please let me tell the whole truth about—you know—*her*."

But Graves frowned, shook his head and passed back a note saying, "You gave me your word!"

So Dalzell, resignedly, gave this bland testimony:

"I met the doctor the day of his arrival, about one o'clock, and except a few minutes between two-thirty and three-thirty was with him all the afternoon. I took lunch with the doctor, and he dined with me. I saw nothing unusual in the doctor's manner. He seemed

148

considerably disturbed at Mrs. Barnaby's death and was sad."

"Did you on that day have a drink of any intoxicating liquor with Dr. Graves?" he was asked.

"One drink of whiskey at Tortoni's."

Cross-examination by Pence followed:

"Did you arrange to go to a ballgame with Dr. Graves?"

"Yes, sir."

"Seemed glad at the chance, did he not?"

"Yes, sir, rather. Said it would lighten up the gloomy day."

"Did you go?"

"No, sir."

"Why not?"

"There was no game."

Laughter.

And Dalzell stepped off the stand, never to tell the truth until too late—long after the trial.

If only at that moment T. J. Dalzell had broken his word to his friend Tom Thatcher Graves, the man who had heroically saved his brother's life way back in the Battle of Antietam! It might have changed the entire course of the trial and verdict. Even then, in those puritanical, God-fearing times, adultery was a lesser crime than murder.

Charles Clinton was then called to the stand.

"I was born in Denver some thirty years ago. I am cashier of the German National Bank. My business requires me to examine handwriting other than signatures."

"You are considered one of the top handwriting experts in the country, are you not?"

"If you choose to say so, Mr. Furman."

Shown the Graves letters and the bottle, and asked if he had seen them before, the witness said he had; two days ago.

"You have examined these letters and the label on this bottle under a microscope. Now will you tell us if you think the same person wrote both that label and the letters?"

149

"I should say the same person did not write them both."

"Can you say by looking at the bottle what the sex of the writer was?"

"Yes."

Doctor Graves and the spectators strained in their seats.

In a stage whisper: "Tell us, please."

"I will say it was unquestionably, a woman."

"A woman?"

"Quite definitely a woman."

A big stir in the courtroom.

Dr. Joseph Bennett, a Denver veterinary surgeon, next took the stand with another good score for the doctor. He said arsenic with potash was a common remedy. It could be found around all livery stables. It was a lotion and was used internally and externally for different reasons. It was used as a lotion to promote healing; in warts and for other purposes. It possessed different degrees of strength used as a lotion, from two to twelve grains. In making this formula no great accuracy was required. After the arsenic dissolved, its strength was easily modified. Dr. Bennett did not think any skill was necessary to compound arsenic and potash.

"Could a woman do it?" asked the defense attorney almost casually.

"Of course," answered the veterinarian.

The defense lawyer smiled.

All in all, a good afternoon for the doctor.

Thirteen

And now it was the doctor's turn, the big day for the star witness in his own defense. How will he stand up against the circumstantial evidence and the pugnacious, high-powered prosecuting attorneys?

When he raised his hand to be sworn, a pallor seemed to spread over Graves' features, but "there was not a trace of nervousness." He looked Clerk Cobbey directly in the eye. In a loud and distinct voice he swore to tell the truth. Sometimes he gave his evidence with hesitation, but usually spoke with conviction. Occasionally a long forefinger pointed toward the jury and from time to time he slammed his fist on the arm of the chair. He confessed that he had no memory for dates, and the jury did not get many. Several times he asked for a question to be repeated. Frequently, he said, almost as a protective device, "It's my impression" or "to the best of my recollection," and his lawyer, fearing the jury's reaction, asked him to be more precise. When he described the series of five meetings at the Barnaby house, he "leaned forward in his chair and alternately fixing his eyes upon the jurors and Mr. Conrad with marked intensity; he gave a graphic and dramatic recital of the events in the library, where his confession is claimed to have been made." The packed courtroom hung on every word. Kitty Graves, who had returned to the courtroom, sat riveted at the attorneys' table and watched the effect of her husband's disclosures on court and jury with her little enigmatic smile.

Dr. Graves was a good witness—at least he had a convincing effect on the spectators. He said he never saw the bottle which contained the poison before it came to Denver. He said he never

151

had any talk with Bennett while swimming, that the interview with Lincoln in the Western Union Telegraph office lasted only a minute, and the one with McHenry and Trickey in his own house not over three minutes. With a knowing smile he denied that he had ever confessed to Conrad and Hanscom that he had sent a bottle of genuine whiskey. He said that the remark he made to Hanscom, that it was "a damned lie," did not refer to the alleged confession, but to Conrad's *claim* that he had made it. Ingenuously, he said:

"Why would I be here fighting for my life if I were the kind of person to so casually confess to such a ghastly crime?"

He accused Conrad, during the interviews when the confession was alleged to have been obtained, of drinking freely. Conrad, he said, had talked to him of his ambition to become United States senator and governor of Montana, and had offered him twenty-five thousand dollars to sign a paper, stating that he had sent a bottle of pure whiskey.

"Interesting," said the defense provocatively, "that he should pick the same sum for a bribe that you were mentioned in the will for."

Then an important piece of evidence was produced:

A receipt for $16,000, given by Mrs. Barnaby to Dr. Graves just before she left for her California trip, was a jolting surprise to the prosecution. This amount would make up a deficiency heretofore unaccounted for between the amount supposed to be in the doctor's hands and the amount of securities turned over. But good was followed by bad when it came out that the book in which Dr. Graves kept all of Mrs. Barnaby's accounts had vanished. Colonel Ballou had gone east and claimed that he made a thorough search in the doctor's office and could find neither the books nor certain papers and letters which had been referred to in the government's evidence. Dr. Graves tried to make a statement to the jury that appearances indicated that the office had been ransacked, presumably by the prosecution's people. It was ruled out after a sharp interchange of insults by Stevens and Judge Macon, in which both

Dr. Graves and the prosecution were charged with doing the ransacking. But, by and large, Graves comported himself well—with dignity and credibility and a beautiful speaking voice. (After all, he was an experienced lecturer on a variety of subjects—the Civil War, travel and religious matters.) At the end of his testimony the audience burst into applause and Judge Rising beat a tattoo with his gavel and swore he would clear the court if it happened again.

Kitty Graves looked happy. Dr. Graves looked confident and pleased. Macon looked smugly around the room as if to say, *"This is your fiendish murderer, gentlemen?"* All was well. But then— then came a bull terrier named "Ikey" Stevens for the cross-examination. Perhaps a ferret would be a better animal to liken him to, for he was small and sleek and darted in and out, inflicting small wounds and waiting patiently for the kill.

For seven straight hours on Saturday Dr. Graves was the target for a relentless and uncompromising cross-examination. Would a lawyer today let his client be hammered at so long and so relentlessly? Especially on petty harassment stuff like this:

Stevens: You went to Providence in 1887?

Graves: About that time.

Q. Can't you remember the year in which you went to Providence? (Raising his arms in exasperation) That ought to be latitude enough?

A. I find it very difficult for me to remember dates or years.

Q. Well, we will give you lots and lots of time to think, Doctor, and if you will kindly tell us the year we would enjoy having it.

A. My recollection is (looking at the ceiling) that it was in 1887.

Q. A.D. or B.C.?

Objection!

Q. All right, in what part of 1887?

A. I commenced going there...

Q. In what part of 1887 did you move to Providence? I cannot put it more simply!

153

A. And, for my part, I cannot say.

Q. Well, was it in the forepart or the middle part or in the latter part, for God's sake!

A. I can't say for sure.

Q. For God's sake, was it in the summer or in the winter?

A. Perhaps—spring.

Q. Your recollection is that it was in the spring? Or was it fall? Was it in April or January or December?

A. I have no recollection.

Q. Can't you give us some sort of a tiny clue or hint as to which month it was?

A. No, sir, I have no recollection. It was almost five years ago, after all.

Q. Then you would not be positive it was in the spring of 1887 you went to Providence, is that right?

A. To the best of my recollection, but I may be entirely mistaken.

Q. Isn't it a fact it was in the latter part of 1887—the fall of the year you went to Providence.

A. I have no recollection whether it was in the spring or in the fall.

On and on, he went, wearing the witness down on the small points, weakening him for the big ones.

And the big ones came soon enough.

Stevens bore in on Graves' trip across the country after learning of Mrs. Barnaby's death. Much badgering about slow trains and fast trains and couldn't he have left sooner from here and why did he delay there and didn't he play cards with some strangers on board? (The beautiful married woman?)

"No, sir," answered Graves a little righteously, "I've never played cards on a train in my life!"

Graves looked his worst in this skirmish—evasive and suffering memory lapses about the simplest things. Of course, if what he

154

told Dalzell about his affair with "the beautiful married woman" en route was true, he *was* lying and hence evasive.

What is hard to understand is why the two relatives he visited weren't subpoenaed, especially in light of this sort of who's-on-first cross-examination. (The prosecution must have certainly verified that he did visit them, no matter how briefly.)

Q. Now, exactly what relationship is this man Williams whom you visited?

A. Cousin.

Q. He is a cousin? Speak up!

A. Cousin.

Q. That is what I asked you! Robert Williams—cousin?

A. Yes.

Q. Whew, we solved that one finally. Now—did you know when you started for Cedar Rapids that he was living there?

A. I did.

Q. You had heard from him, I imagine?

A. Not directly.

Q. But you heard from him indirectly, before you left Providence?

A. No, sir.

Q. Did you notify him you were going to stop off at Cedar Rapids?

A. No, sir.

Q. Didn't tell him you would be there and pay him a visit?

A. No, sir.

Q. Nor to your uncle at Sterling?

A. No, sir.

Q. It was a sort of impromptu visit you decided upon when you arrived in Chicago?

A. Yes, or as I was running into Chicago.

Q. Just before you reached Chicago you decided upon this?

A. I thought if I could I would.

Q. Just descend upon them—like that?

A. Yes, sir.

Q. And you made no inquiries about the train for Denver, but started for Sterling and Cedar Rapids?

A. If I did I had forgotten it. I was half sick and I didn't—

Q. Now were you ill when you arrived at Sterling?

A. I was.

Q. Were you worse than when you left Chicago?

A. I can't say.

Q. Don't you remember?

A. No, sir.

Q. Don't you remember saying something to your uncle about feeling very badly?

A. I did; they urged me to stay.

Q. Didn't you take some medicine there?

A. I did not.

Q. Did you feel well or ill when you got to Sterling station?

A. Decidedly ill.

Q. What kind of weather, was it pleasant weather?

A. Very muddy.

Q. Roads very muddy, eh?

A. Yes.

Q. Quite damp, eh?

A. The roads were very muddy.

Q. Been storming that day?

A. I can't say so.

Q. Hadn't it been storming recently?

A. I can't say so.

Q. Weren't the roads covered with snow?

A. No, sir.

Q. How do you remember it was very muddy?

A. From the fact that it was difficult for the horses to draw the carriage.

Q. You noticed along the road as you went down to Sterling,

looking out of the window, that the roads were in pretty bad condition?

A. No, sir.

Q. Not until you got to Sterling, then you found your uncle lived six miles in the country, and you hired a carriage to take you out?

A. I knew before I got there he had lived six miles in the country; I had heard through my mother for twenty years from him.

Q. You never heard from him directly?

A. I never received a letter from him if that's what you mean.

Q. Had you ever seen him in your life?

A. I had.

Q. How long before?

A. Nearly thirty years.

Q. Before—you were not intimate acquaintances?

A. As intimate as any young man would be with his uncle.

Q. You never visited him at Sterling?

A. I lived with his family at Sterling thirty years before for a time.

Q. Then when you returned to Sterling you were feeling very much better, is that right?

A. No, for I was sick in the station, quite sick.

Q. Then the trip didn't do you any good, is that right?

A. Well, possibly it did.

Q. It helped you going out and hurt you coming back, is that it?

A. Possibly.

Q. You were sick when you arrived in Sterling?

A. Yes.

Q. And that made you decide to go on to Cedar Rapids?

A. Yes.

Q. And thinking, of course, being with a cousin, if you were going to be sick, it would be better than being with strangers, is that right?

A. Yes.

Q. That was your reason for stopping over at Cedar Rapids. How long did you stay there?

A. I stayed until eight-forty at night; eight-forty in the evening, that was the first train, the first through train, so my cousin informed me, that I could take.

Q. The first through train to Denver?

A. Yes sir. That is, I was informed by my cousin that the train— the tickets that I held—would not go until eight-forty that evening.

Q. But if you had been informed by the station agent in Sterling, Illinois, that you could have waited about three hours longer and could have taken the flyer, which would have landed you in Denver Thursday morning, you still would not have done that because you were determined to stop off at Cedar Rapids?

A. I had no conversation with him.

Q. If you had known it would not have made any difference. You had made up your mind to stop at Cedar Rapids?

A. I don't know what I should have done.

Q. Anyhow, you didn't have the information, or didn't ask for it?

A. That is it.

Q. And you went to Cedar Rapids and stopped until eight-forty-five in the evening?

A. Yes.

Q. And then you took the slow train for Denver?

A. I don't know whether it was slow or fast.

Q. Did you come fast or slow to Denver?

A. No, sir.

Q. What do you mean, no sir? Did it stop at every station?

A. I don't remember anything about it.

Q. Have no recollection of that at all?

A. No, sir.

Q. You haven't a very good memory, have you?

A. No, sir.

158

Q. And it didn't make any difference whether the train was slow or fast, according to your recollection?

A. I should have been pleased had it been fast. I don't know whether it was slow or fast.

Q. Let me show you. This, sir, is fast (moves hand past his face quickly) and this, sir, might be considered slow (moves his hand across his face slowly). See the difference? Now—there is no impression left on your mind, one way or the other?

A. No, sir.

Q. I'm worried about you, sir. You could be suffering from amnesia?

Objection! Badgering!

Sustained.

Q. You made some friends on the train, or those who became your friends?

A. I made some what one might call car acquaintances.

Q. That's what I mean, car acquaintances. They were your friends while you were traveling?

A. We spoke.

Q. Of course, I don't understand your distinction between friends and acquaintances. I presume you can explain. Do you mean to say they didn't know you long enough so you could draw a will for them, and have one drawn, and appoint you their agent with full power to act and see that you were mentioned heavily in the aforementioned will?

Objection!

Objection!

A. That wasn't discussed, sir.

Hour after hour the harangue went on, with Graves gamely counter-punching the vicious jabs of the bantamweight Stevens but rarely landing a solid blow. After this exchange he received a small, but sorely needed round of applause from the audience:

159

Q. You were surprised to learn that Mrs. Conrad was in Denver?

A. Yes. I thought she'd be in her home in Montana or back in Providence for the funeral.

Q. You probably showed that surprise?

A. No doubt but that I did.

Q. You might have given half a spring or something of that kind out of your chair, because it was a surprise to you, wasn't it?

A. A marked surprise.

Q. There is no doubt about that! And you might have exhibited the feeling that Mrs. Worrell described?

A. I exhibited surprise.

Q. And may have done it in the way she described?

A. She exaggerated.

Q. Well, but in some such way?

A. I expressed surprise.

Q. Well, you were feeling troubled at that time, weren't you? Of course you were! You can't recollect what you did. You have frequently stated that time and again. Shocked, you may have jumped half out of your chair?

A. I did not do that!

Q. You remember that distinctly?

A. I do! I don't jump out of chairs!

Q. Astonishing, you have an excellent memory for some things. And you remember the things which occurred under great excitement and stress of mind better than you do when you are cool and calm—is that right?

A. No, sir.

Q. But, of course, you were suffering at this time; you had been informed of the terrible cause of death—such a *surprise* to you that death—and were agitated and distressed and nervous, weren't you?

A. I was.

Q. When you were informed that the murdered woman's daughter was there, you remember distinctly you didn't jump out of your chair and make a start?

A. I may have made a slight start.

Q. But you think Mrs. Worrell exaggerated in her description?

A. Why else was she brought here to testify, sir?

Applause in the courtroom.

The next day Graves again scored a minor point—not on facts, unfortunately, but simply by his cool and gentle delivery:

Q. And you spent the entire day from the time you left Mr. Worrell's office with the esteemed Mr. Dalzell. Is that right?

A. Up to the time, or nearly the time of the leaving of the train.

Q. And you went out driving, and wanted to go to a ball game, and took a drink at the Tortoni? He took lunch with you, and you took dinner with him?

A. Yes.

Q. And yet during none of this time did you even attempt to find out specifics with reference to the poisoning which had been administered to Mrs. Barnaby, the examination the doctors had of the bottle, the autopsy, the embalming, or to see the physician in attendance, or anything except what you have related. Is that right?

A. It had all been done. I am a doctor, not a mortician nor a detective nor a policeman nor a necrophiliac.

Q. A what?

A. Sir, you do have a dictionary, I suppose?

Q. Well, we can't all be Harvard men, can we.

A. Pity.

Laughter in the courtroom.

Q. Getting back, learned doctor, this dead woman is one of the best friends you ever had in the world?

A. That is correct.

Q. And your benefactress?

161

A. Yes.

Q. She came to you when you needed somebody just like her?

A. No, sir.

Q. What do you mean by benefactress then?

A. Well, I don't know exactly how to express it.

Q. What is a benefactress, as you call it?

A. A person to whom you are under some obligation, who aids your career.

Q. Is that all?

(Yes, indeed *was* that all? Mightn't the doctor have been romantically involved with the comely widow Barnaby, a woman who liked a naughty joke and a whiskey? Mightn't a transaction of a less revolting nature have taken place in the doctor's study on one of her many "secret" visits? The audience and jury were certainly thinking along those lines).

A. That confers in some manner or other benefits upon you.

Q. *Great* benefits and favors, is that right, my dear doctor?

A. The adjective you may insert, sir.

Q. When you expressed yourself time and again that she was your benefactress—what did you mean exactly?

A. I meant that Mrs. Barnaby and myself were good friends.

Q. That is all you meant?

A. Yes.

Q. Then why, for God's sake, didn't you say simply, "she was a good friend of mine?"

A. Simply, sir, because I used the other word.

Q. You wrote a letter to Mrs. Conrad, didn't you?

A. I did.

Q. And you hadn't seen anything about what occurred in the Western Union office in any newspaper, had you?

A. I think at the time I wrote the letter to Mrs. Conrad I had seen it.

162

Q. I asked you if you ever had seen it, Dr. Graves! I asked you if you had ever seen it in any newspaper and you said no! Never! Remember that little detail? Never?

A. I misunderstood your question!

Q. Then as a matter of fact you did see this published in the newspapers, didn't you? What was said in the Western Union office?

A. I don't think I read it, but I think my mother or family told me. I don't think I read it myself, for I would not read the papers.

Q. You were so frightened that you would not read the papers?

A. I was not frightened! I was simply disgusted; normally I didn't read the papers very often.

Q. In this letter to Mrs. Conrad, you say "on my return to Providence I found my wife had been decoyed away by a bogus telegram. Under great excitement I rushed to the telegraph office, hardly knowing what I did in my distress of mind; I was betrayed into saying some indiscreet words; to my horror I found columns of stuff in the papers," and so forth?

A. Yes, sir.

Q. Then you must have read the papers!

A. I didn't read it! My mother told me—and I asked her in a general way about it!

Q. Then how do you know whether the papers told the truth or whether they were false, if she only told you in a quote general way unquote?

A. (Exasperated) Simply because what she told me I said was false.

Q. What paper did she call your attention to?

A. I can't say.

Q. Was it the Boston *Herald?*

A. I would not have it in the house, a nasty, low paper.

Q. Isn't it the leading newspaper in New England?

A. Hardly!

Q. Now deferring to your opinion, the cause of your feeling

163

Lafe Pence
Stevens' handsome deputy

Judge Amos Rising
The trial judge

against the *Herald* is that it refused at one time to publish one of your advertisements?

A. That is a lie, sir.

Q. That they exclude all sort of medicine advertisements? Is not that the cause of your feeling?

A. Not at all! Ever since I was a boy I have been opposed to the Boston *Herald*.

Q. What did it say about you when you were a boy, Graves?

Defense lawyers jumped up in unison. Objection! Sustained.

And the ferret went on undaunted to attack and chew very successfully. We are now in his third day of his inquisition and Graves is ashen with fatigue and sweaty and visibly confused. Stevens, small and dapper and cool, looks as though the fight has just begun. Indeed, it is ending rapidly, and as Graves wilts Stevens blossoms.

Q. You saw this letter which was sent to Mrs. Conrad is dated on the thirtieth of April, 1891, and you arrived in Providence on the twenty-seventh, didn't you?

A. Well, I can't remember dates; it is utterly impossible.

Q. You don't remember that you got home?

A. I remember that, but to remember dates is utterly impossible. I have got one date fixed in my mind, and that is when I was born, and that is the only date I am sure of right now.

Q. You refresh your mind from the family Bible every once in a while on that date?

A. I have been absent some time, and lately I haven't seen it.

Q. Has it been stolen in Providence also?

Objection! Sarcastic badgering.

Dr. Graves turned shakily to the judge. "Your honor, I am getting tired. Would you be so kind as to let me off until two o'clock simply as a matter of rest for me? My brain is tired, in a turmoil."

The court: "We will take a recess now."

The court took a recess until two o'clock.

According to Furman's memoirs, Graves and Furman hurried out the side door- and went to Tortoni's. The elegant restaurant was crowded and the owner, Enrico, and the customers looked up and hushed when they saw the two men come in through the elaborately engraved glass doors. T. Thatcher Graves was now a bigger celebrity in Denver than even Senator Tabor and the flamboyant Baby Doe. As they walked past the tables with the flower vases and white tablecloths, several people clapped Graves on the back and said such things as "Good luck, doctor!" and "Give the little bastard hell!" And "You'll win out, Tom!"

Graves nodded to them courteously and murmured "Thank you, thank you." He was moved and grateful.

They entered a booth and drew a curtain. Graves sank down on the bench and, gray of face, leaned back with an exhausted sigh. "My poor Kitty. If I were only guilty, I would take her and flee to Canada tonight!"

"Don't talk like that, Tom. We're doing all right, you'll see. But you must cut down on your 'I thinks' and 'to the best of my recollections' and 'my impression is.' That little rat is making hay with that."

"But he gets me all rattled—I can't remember my own name!"

"Take your time before answering. Then just tell the truth."

"You're right—you're right."

"That note Dalzell sent you—anything we might use?"

Graves shook his head. Just then the curtain was jerked open. A paunchy man in a morning coat stood there swaying, a glass of champagne in his hand. He raised his glass and slurred: "Here's hoping you swing for it, you damned charlatan!"

Furman jumped up, his fist drawn back, but Graves restrained

165

him: "Who knows, sir—we just might oblige you," Graves said with an ironic smile.

Then after a virtually untouched lunch, they went back to the courtroom. And more relentless pick-pick-pick.

Q. How long, my good doctor, have you known Mr. Bennett, Edward Bennett?

A. Would you kindly not call me your good doctor—any more than I shall call you my good executioner?

Q. Well, how long?

A. I became acquainted with him in the Adirondacks at the time we went to the Adirondacks, the only time.

Q. That was in August 1880, wasn't it, that you were there?

A. Yes.

Q. See how you're improving, doctor? You actually got a date right! Good fellow! Keep it up now!

A. I'm doing the best I can, sir.

Q. I'm *sure* you are. Now—that was the extent of your acquaintance with Mr. Bennett?

A. Yes.

Q. You said, I think—that is, *it is my impression,* to your counsel, that you always found him straightforward and an honorable man with you; that is correct, isn't it? I mean, to the best of your recollection?

A. Yes, sir.

Q. And you formed some sort of high opinion for him and therefore he got this letter of recommendation?

A. As a guide, I was perfectly satisfied with him.

Q. You thought he understood his business most excellently well?

A. He does; no better guide in the mountains.

Q. Not in the woods?

A. I said in the mountains. But also in the woods, if you wish.

Q. And you thought very highly of him as a man, didn't you?

166

A. Just a moment now—I didn't know enough about him to form...

Q. One way or the other, then, you have expressed an opinion about him one way or the other.

A. I think I have.

Q. You have expressed an opinion adversely to him, haven't you?

A. Simply that he was—

Q. Answer the question please, sir! You were doing so well there for a while!

A. Yes, sir... He was a drunkard.

Q. I think I asked you this question as to what the home of the Bennetts was called, or what that portion of the Adirondacks where you were stopping was called, and you never heard it called "The Woods."

A. I probably heard it called "The Woods." Don't you understand, everything there by everyone was called "The Woods"!

Q. You yourself—you never called it "The Woods"?

A. I might have. I probably did. Everyone did.

Q. To refresh your memory let me—You told me this morning very positively you had not, is that true or not?

A. I was under the impression your question referred to the expression "in the woods."

Q. You'd heard *that* expression?

A. Probably I have. Certainly. Since childhood. Witches, goblins—all "in the woods."

Q. Well, I asked you specifically about that this morning. Now isn't it a fact that at the time you were in the mountains that it was a common expression with reference to that section of the country, and when they spoke of people up there they said, "Your friends in the woods," or the "people who live in the woods," or something of that kind?

A. I never heard of it in that particular sense. What is the difference?

167

Q. You never heard it?

A. My impression—my best recollection is—

Upon using the verboten phrases, Graves sent his lawyer a stricken look, like a prizefighter caught on the ropes looking at his corner for help. Stevens tried not to look smug and relentlessly pressed on:

Q. My, you are pretty positive, aren't you.

A. I may have heard it, but damn it, it made no impression upon me sufficient for me to recollect!

Q. So, you never used the expression yourself?

A. I may have used it.

Q. Never heard it used?

A. I may have! Is there anyone in the world who at one time or another has not said that something or someone was in the woods!

Q. Did you use it in your conversation with Mr. Bennett?

A. No, sir; no occasion to.

Q. Did you ever use it in any letter to Mrs. Barnaby?

A. I don't know.

Q. Or to Mr. Bennett?

A. I do not know.

Q. What is your, you know, your "best impression"?

A. I have no impression upon the subject.

Q. What is the best of your "recollection"?

A. I have no recollection upon the subject.

Graves' lawyer jumped up. "Your honor, this is badgering, pure and simple!"

Overruled!

Q. If you did use it, did you not pick it up during your trip there in the mountains?

A I don't know!

Q. In the letter of September 4, 1890 (holding it up) which you wrote to Mr. Bennett, and wrote as a recommendation to him. I will ask you if you didn't use this kind of language: "Of course, it is hardly necessary for me to say that which everyone in the woods knows as a fact," and so forth.

A. That is my writing.

Q. And you must have been familiar with that kind of expression?

A. Obviously, as I wrote it.

Q. So you did use it on that one occasion?

A. I obviously did.

Q. I will ask you whether or not in any one of your letters to Mrs. Barnaby you used that kind of expression?

A. I might have. I don't know. Is it that unusual an expression?

Q. You have heard the expression used, haven't you, as relating to these people who live in the Adirondacks?

A. Obviously I didn't invent those three words. They're in the dictionary.

Judge Rising: "I'm getting bored with this!"

Furman: "And so say we all!"

Stevens, also weary of the game, finally changed the subject, leaving the witness nearly mincemeat. Stevens gave Graves a few moments to dab his brow with a handkerchief and then he took another tack.

Q. Mrs. Barnaby was under your care and came to your house where your office was very frequently used for treatment?

A. She did.

Q. Speak up, sir. And she came when your wife was there?

A. My wife was always there when she was there, unless she was out making calls!

Q. And your treatment was administered in the presence of your wife?

A. Always.

Q. Didn't you keep a stub book, did you not keep a record of your checks? On the stubs as you would give them?

A. I did, but the stub book is gone.

Q. What a pity! Do you know where it is?

A. No, sir, I do not.

Q. You have no idea?

A. No, sir. Everything went when my office was ransacked by your people!

Graves' rare burst of anger produced consternation in the court. Then Stevens nipped cruelly: "Now careful, sir, or your nose will grow like Pinocchio's."

Much gavel rapping by the judge, until Stevens got back on course.

Q. Did you used to make checks out in favor of Mrs. Worrell?

A. I did.

Q. And send to Mrs. Barnaby addressed to Mrs. Barnaby. You said you had received a salary of twenty-five hundred dollars a year?

A. It was the understanding between Mrs. Barnaby and myself.

Q. Did you receive it?

A. I did.

Q. When did you draw it?

A. It was figured in at the time, sixteenth of December, figured up to that date.

Q. Look how your dates are improving, sir! Now, for how many years?

A. Simply for what was due up to that time.

Q. How much was due up to that time?

A. I could not tell you without reference to my books. As you know, the books are lost or, rather, stolen.

Q. Colonel Ballou has not been able to find them, or you?

A. I have not searched for them; as you know, I've been here in Denver, otherwise occupied. Colonel Ballou and his partner and his office boy have searched for them.

Q. And they haven't found them?

A. They could not find them. You know all this, sir!

Q. Just could not find them, eh? I must warn you, sir, that I have a very suspicious nature.

A. And I must warn you, sir, that I have a very clear conscience.

Applause.
Silence!

Q. I wish you would recall. You went over this matter with Mrs. Barnaby, how much of that sixteen thousand dollars is your salary?

A. I don't know.

Q. How were you in the habit of drawing your salary?

A. Well, I could hardly say that. I don't think you understand— I could have drawn out all of her money at any time I chose to, just as I could have killed her any time I chose to! I simply didn't choose to!

Q. I will ask you if it is not a fact that you were in the habit of drawing money from these funds just as you needed it?

A. I don't understand you.

Q. I think the question is plain. Weren't you in the habit of drawing money from Mrs. Barnaby's funds as you needed it for yourself?

A. No, sir. But I certainly could have had I wished.

Q. How did you draw it?

A. I should have to qualify that by saying that some of that was reckoned on my salary at the time of the settlement.

Q. On December twenty-second you drew one hundred and ten dollars?

A. I don't know.

Q. You don't know whether you did or didn't?

A. I don't know.

171

Stevens marched to the exhibits table and picked up a piece of paper, then turned delicately on his heel to flourish it.

Q. Would this statement refresh your memory, do you think?

In spite of himself, Graves found his eyes following the paper in Stevens' hand as it moved in the air.

A. I don't know anything about that statement.
Q. It is a certified statement from your bank.
A. Well, then it is.
Q. The seventh of January, didn't you draw three hundred dollars?
A. Look sir, you have the statement in your hand. If it says I did, then I did.

Judge Furman stood up. "Your Honor, my client is not an embezzler and is not on trial for it. He is on trial for murder. Can we stick to that issue?"
Objection.
Overruled.
Stevens bore in like a dentist's drill.

Q. February second. I will ask you if you didn't draw one hundred dollars?
A. I don't know.
Q. I will ask you if on the twenty-third of February you didn't draw three hundred dollars?
A. I don't know. Look at the statement.
Q. I will ask you if on March eleventh you didn't draw one hundred dollars?
A. I don't know. It's all there.
Q. I will ask you if on March twenty-third you didn't draw two hundred and fifty dollars?

A. I don't know.

Q. I will ask you if on April 7, 1891, you didn't draw ten thousand dollars?

A. I don't know about the date, but I drew ten thousand dollars.

Q. And placed it to your own credit in another bank?

A. I turned it over to the appointed Mr. Van Slyck, as was proper!

Q. You state that at the time this settlement was made, you took Mrs. Barnaby into your office and went over those account books with her?

A. Mrs. Barnaby came into my office. I didn't take her there... she came into my office, and we did go over the accounts carefully, spent two hours nearly.

It was now two antagonists, no longer questioner and respondent, district attorney and defendant but adversaries who had assumed distinct roles, personae. Stevens the man versus Graves the man.

Stevens: And you went over these accounts?

Graves: We did—very, very carefully.

Stevens: You found Mrs. Barnaby a great care to you, didn't you?

Graves: Care?

Stevens: Problem. Quite a handful?

Graves: I hardly know how to answer that.

Stevens: Caused you a great deal of trouble to look after her affairs?

Graves: I hardly know how to answer that. At times it would.

Stevens: You went and collected these rents from the tenement houses sometimes?

Graves: Whenever Mrs. Barnaby was in Providence she collected them.

Stevens: But she was generally away from there while you were her agent?

Graves: She liked to collect them whenever she was in town, and did so.

Stevens: But most of the time you had to collect the rents?

Graves: Yes.

Stevens: And it was a great source of annoyance to have to collect them?

Graves: It was not.

Stevens: It was a pleasure?

Graves: It was neither pleasure nor annoyance, it was business with me. What in the world are you driving at?

Stevens: At the same time you had all you could do in your profession?

Graves: I was a very busy man, and always have been.

Stevens: In your profession?

Graves: Every way. Charity work, war veteran work, lecturing, church work, and of course my profession.

Stevens: Your profession?

Graves: My profession! Sir, what in the world are you after?

Stevens: But you were willing to go into the business management game, and did go into it for her and did serve her. Is that right?

Graves: I did.

Stevens: Why?

Graves: Why?

Stevens: Yes, why? (leaning forward, a fellow conspirator): Love for the old girl, pity for the old thing, and a chance to make a monetary killing while treating her with placebos?

Objection! Objection!

Sustained.

Stevens (with a calmer approach): Did you ever compound anything that compounded arsenite or potassium?

Graves: No recollection of it.

174

Stevens: Never use arsenic in any of your medicines?

Graves: I use Fowler's Solution. Every other physician does.

Stevens: And, of course, you know how that is compounded.

Graves: I do.

Stevens. And you have compounded it yourself?

Graves: No, I don't think I ever made any Fowler's Solution. One can buy it so easily.

A good point here. In fact, a number of courtroom spectators would have had Fowler's Solution in their own stables, since it was in common usage for horse as well as human care.

Stevens: But you know its uses?

Graves: Every physician uses it.

Stevens: And they use it quite frequently?

Graves: It would depend upon your practice; some use it more than others.

Stevens: And you are in the habit of using it?

Graves: If it is called for I use it.

Stevens: Are you in the habit of using anything stronger?

Graves: What do you mean?

Stevens: Anything containing more arsenic than Fowler's Solution?

Graves: It would be very simple to make Fowler's stronger— say, for treating a horse—if one wanted to.

Stevens: Never use it in your practice?

Graves: I never use any preparation of arsenic except Fowler's Solution, and an ounce would last me a long time.

Not making headway here, Stevens went back to familiar territory: character defamation.

Stevens: On the morning that Mr. McHenry and Trickey were at your house did you say anything about Mrs. Barnaby's affairs?

175

Graves: I don't think I did.

Stevens: Didn't they ask you, "What impression did you form of the Bennetts?"

Graves: No, sir.

Stevens: Didn't you answer, "Bennett is a loafer; he and his wife are getting a good deal out of Mrs. Barnaby, and he is continually getting drunk with her"?

Graves: I certainly did not, nothing of the kind.

Stevens: "Often they went out to an icehouse and drank together"?

Graves: That is positively false.

Stevens: The other answer is not so *positively* false?

Graves: Yes sir, it is.

Stevens: I will help you: Did anyone ever come to you and say in Providence that they saw Edward Bennett there or elsewhere repeatedly drunk or half drunk?

Graves: I don't recollect.

Stevens: That his reputation at Blue Mountain was that of a common drunkard. Did anyone ever tell you that in Providence?

Graves: I don't recollect.

Stevens: Did you learn that while you were on this trip in the Blue Mountains?

Graves: That is putting it rather strong, except when he was drunk.

Stevens: Do you know whose language it is?

Graves: Yes.

Stevens: It is your own!

Graves: I use strong language sometimes.

Stevens: Is that true or false?

Graves: That he did get drunk?

Stevens: No, sir; that he was not a suitable person for a lady to be with?

Graves: I could hardly say in relation to that at the present time.

Mr. Bennett's thirst and conduct are not my responsibility and never have been.

Stevens: You first told Mr. Anthony that Bennett was a loafer and drunkard, and wasn't a suitable person for a lady to be with, and then you told him it was all true, and now you say it was not true; is that right?

Is there no end to the harangue? Where, I find myself asking, did Stevens learn to do this? Strange were the tools of justice then—almost as strange as today—and men were hardly just in their means. From here on in, it might just as well have been verbal badminton played by nameless contestants.

That is about what you told Anthony?

In substance, but Bennett is not a loafer.

He is not a drunkard, is he?

He comes as close as you can to that description without being in an institution.

You remember the letter that you gave to Mr. Bennett?

Yes.

Didn't you tell Judge Furman yesterday that he was a most excellent guide?

Yes.

Can a drunkard be a most excellent guide?

Yes, when sober.

Doctor, prior to the time you met Mr. Conrad on these nights, had you taken any steps to find out who the murderer was of Mrs. Barnaby?

I considered the matter out of my hands.

Then you had not taken any steps to find out?

I'm not a detective.

Did Sallie Hanley ever write to you about Mrs. Barnaby being out riding one day and a storm coming up and she and Mr. Bennett landed on an island where there was an old icehouse, and they had to stay there until after the storm' had subsided?

No recollection of it.

She may have written you such a letter?

I never heard of it before.

Your best recollection?

I never saw any such letter, and never heard of it before.

Did you receive such information from her, either before or since that time?

No, sir.

Is not that the origin of all this disgusting talk about the icehouse at Blue Mountain Lake?

I don't know anything about it.

You don't? You don't?

No, sir.

Nothing at all?

Furman intercepts, rescuing the harassed witness: "I don't think I care to re-examine Dr. Graves! That is all, doctor, I am satisfied with your cross-examination."

Kitty Graves is next called to the stand, God knows for what purpose, for she is asked absolutely nothing of importance by the defense. And Stevens—the bulldog—declines to cross-examine!

Here is her testimony in its vapid entirety. Don't look for any clues here, but it's important because it is the first time we hear her voice, no matter how bland. Perhaps the blandness *is* a clue.

She takes the witness stand looking fragile but exquisite, her dark, slightly wild eyes "burning into whomever they fasten on," her cupid bow mouth curved down in one corner, slightly up in the other à la Gioconda, her dove-wing hat tipped rakishly, and answers the questions in a demure, quiet voice—such a rarefied accent for a middle-class woman!

178

There is not a sound in the courtroom. Will she be asked the question, "Did your husband murder Mrs. Barnaby?" Or, "Did *you* murder Mrs. Barnaby?" Or, "Do you know who murdered Mrs. Barnaby?" Or, "Who do you think murdered Mrs. Barnaby?"

If the crowded courtroom thought they might get these titillating questions—with or without answers—they were out of luck.

Instead they heard from the defense the following:

"How long ago did you become acquainted with Mrs. Barnaby?"

"Three years."

"Do you remember when your husband became Mrs. Barnaby's agent?"

"Yes, sir."

"You were in the Adirondacks a year ago last summer?"

"Yes, sir."

"Did she endeavor to get any member of your family to go to California with her?"

"Yes, sir; she wanted my husband to go."

"Before she received the letter from Mrs. Worrell, had either you or your husband promised to go?"

"No, sir.

"Was anything said about a European trip?"

"Yes, sir; for the next summer." (With a girlish smile) "We were certainly looking forward to it!"

Mr. Furman then showed Mrs. Graves the power of attorney given her husband, and she said it was the original one and that her husband read it to Mrs. Barnaby.

"Where were you when your husband received the telegram announcing Mrs. Barnaby's illness?"

"At my father's house in Newton."

"What time did he get it?"

"About one o'clock."

"What did the doctor do upon receipt of it?"

179

"He said he must go to her, and left that afternoon."

They discussed Mr. Conrad and the nightly sessions in the Barnaby mansion.

"I saw Mr. Conrad the next night, Sunday, and asked again about his wife, and was told she was still ill. My husband went with him again that night."

"Did you see Mr. Conrad again?"

"No sir, but I heard him call at the door and speak to my husband. The doctor told him he was going to Denver, and Mr. Conrad said: 'That's good, my man, I'll go with you!' My husband said, 'I am not your man' and that he preferred to go alone, and shut the door in his face."

"Were you at home on Thursday night when your husband returned?"

"Yes, sir."

"What was his humor?"

"He was very angry."

"Are you the wife of the defendant?"

"I am, sir."

At this point Graves had a heated, whispered discussion with his lawyer.

And then—Mrs. Graves was excused.

There was no cross-examination by the district attorney.

And that is it. Never has such an important witness been so wasted by both sides.

Why?

It is inexplicable. For example, why didn't the defense ask at least one heavy, emotional question at the end, such as "Mrs. Graves, I ask you, did your husband kill Mrs. Barnaby?"

Think of the effect on the jury if she had turned those enigmatic eyes on them and given a smile and said, in that little girl voice: "Why, everyone who knows my Tom knows he couldn't hurt a fly!"

I can come up with no explanation either for the opportunistic Mr. Stevens not leaping at the chance for cross-examination. Ex-

180

cept: perhaps she was inviolate, unassailable since her beauty, decorum and fey charm seemed to have captured all Denver; if he had tried his bullying tactics on her, they might have backfired. (Remember, it was not well known at this point that she had had a long history of mental problems. Or did Stevens lay off her for that very reason?)

But think of how many points the defense could have scored with her! What a splendid husband and son Graves was, how he visited his parents every Sunday, how hard he worked, how he never said anything bad about Mrs. Barnaby, no matter how difficult the old girl was; how he would work and worry about her portfolio of investments far into the night, and so on.

To me it's one of the biggest enigmas of the case.

The other one that nags at me is why neither Kitty or Dr. Graves was asked if they were in Boston the day the bottle was mailed; and, if not, what their alibis were. It seems so fundamental.

Now, as we are winding down in the trial, along comes a delight, one E. R. Bertram, a refreshing blithe spirit who does nothing for the defense but does a great deal for comic relief. He is a short, purple-nosed leprechaun who was obviously brought in by the defense to bolster their shaky notion that since the fatal bottle spent one night in the buggy in the Empire Stables before Mrs. Barnaby drank it, it could well have been emptied of real whiskey and poison substituted. It strikes me as an egregious error on Furman's and Macon's part to have let Mr. Bertram anywhere near the courtroom and in striking distance of Stevens, who had a field day.

Bertram, wearing high boots and red suspenders, did all right under the defense's rational and brief questioning; but then Stevens took over.

It became, in short order, high vaudeville and the audience howled.

One could almost see Stevens mentally rubbing his hands as he sauntered up to the red-faced and, as yet, unintimidated witness.

"Where are you employed?"

"Who?"

"You, sir. Employed."

"Oh, at the Empire Stables."

"What is your business?"

"What business?"

"What do you do?"

"I'm a groom, I'm in that business."

"Do you know Dan Smith?"

"Dan! I do, I do. He's the fellow who told me that he'd taken a drink out of the bottle!"

"What bottle?"

"Well, you know," (behind his hand as though it were a secret) "the one that's caused all the commotion. And he said that it would not hurt a baby."

"What were his exact words?"

"Those were them!"

Laughter.

"Your father lives in Hartford?"

"Yes."

"Business?"

"Miller."

"Flour mill?"

"Saw mill."

Laughter.

"When did you come to Colorado?"

"Year ago last May."

"Where did you come from?"

"Chicago."

"What did you do there?"

"Nothing."

"If you did nothing, how'd you get arrested?"

(Shocked) "How'd you know I was arrested?"

"What did you do to get arrested?"

182

"None of your business, if I might say so, sir."

Laughter.

"In jail?"

"Yes, sir."

"Ever arrested since?"

"May have been. Possibly."

"What name did you give the police?"

"E. R. Bertram. I am totally honest with them always."

"Didn't you give the name Murray?"

"No, sir, not the first time."

"Wasn't your picture taken and put in the rogues' gallery as Murray?"

"Don't rightly know about that."

"Now, come on, be a good fellow, what were you arrested for?"

"There was a non-substantial charge of obtaining some goods under false pretenses, sir."

"Why didn't you say so a while ago?"

(Offended) "Why should I?"

"What refreshed your recollection?"

(Loftily) "I didn't think there was any need of avoiding that there question!"

"So, back to jail?"

"City jail."

"How long?"

"Couple of days. Well, week or two."

"Month or two?"

"You might say."

"Who had you arrested?"

"A man named Allen."

"Who arrested you just before Christmas?"

"I don't remember."

"Longman?"

"Can't say. Sounds familiar."

"City officer?"

"I think so. Looked like one."

"Who had you arrested before that?"

"A man named Delaney. Nice fellow."

"What did he have you arrested for?"

"Not paying my board, and I'll tell you he didn't get his board either!"

"What were you arrested for before?"

(Hurt) "I was never arrested but three times in my life!"

"What! Do you mean to tell the jury that you have lived here nearly two years and have only been arrested three times?"

"That's what I do, sir, and I'm a man of my word!"

"How many times were you arrested in Chicago when you were there six weeks?"

(More mulish than sheepish) "I told you that I was never arrested but three times in my life."

"Why didn't you say so at first then?"

"Don't have to."

Laughter.

"Now, when you talked with Smith about this, when was it?"

"Twice. Four months ago and a week before he testified."

"Just a week?"

"I can't say exactly."

"What date was it?"

"I don't know."

"Was it before Thanksgiving?"

"Thanksgiving's like any other day to me."

"Weren't you out of jail then?"

"Damn right I was out of jail then!"

"Tell us just what he told you?"

"Who?"

A fat woman in the back row was laughing so hard that she collapsed into uncontrollable coughing and had to be helped from the courtroom by the bailiff.

Stevens, smiling but raising his shoulders in exasperation: "Dan Smith, sir, Dan Smith—that's who we're talking about!"

"He said he took the package out of the buggy and opened it and took a drink out of it. 'Looky, not bad,' he says, 'wouldn't hurt a kid.'"

Laughter.

"Didn't he say 'baby'?"

"He said kid."

"You told Mr. Furman he said baby."

"Well, they both come under the same thing, don't they?"

The court threatened to have the room cleared if there was any more laughter.

"How much cash have you?"

"Is that any of your business?"

"It is."

"Well, I have seventy-five cents."

"Any expectations of getting more?"

"No, sir, not right this moment."

"Whom did you first tell this?"

"Jimmie White."

"When did you tell him?"

"Four or five days ago."

"Waited ten days?"

"I did."

"Didn't it occur to you that an innocent man might be hanged as a result of the lack of that testimony?"

"That's the reason I told it. Poor devil shouldn't hang for want of some simple honest testimony, right?"

"Right, sir."

(Stevens clearing his throat and growing serious) "Now Mr. Bertram—"

"That's me."

185

"Do you know what perjury is?"

"Yes, sir."

"Ever been convicted of perjury?"

(Indignant) "I have not, sir, and I don't intend to be!"

Dismissed.

Alas, I would have liked to have seen a great deal more of Mr. Bertram, but off he went to a destiny unknown. I would have liked to have seen him brought in at regular intervals, periodically, like Bottom or Falstaff, if only to lighten these turgid proceedings.

I submit that a night club team could incorporate that exchange into its act—verbatim from the court transcript—with considerable success.

But a man's life was at stake, there was nothing comic about it, and sadly, Mr. Bertram's little moment on stage was the last bit of humor in Graves' long trial.

I wonder if Mr. Bertram's testimony and character didn't ultimately hurt the case for the defense—he was so palpably in the pocket of the defense, so obviously bribed to testify—or, should one say, promised a fine "reward"—that though the jury laughed, didn't they chalk up some bad marks for Graves?

Two other stablemen—nonclowns this time—also testified for the defense, saying that they had seen the fatal bottle in the buggy in the stable.

It was almost all over. But suddenly a last bit of physical evidence was introduced by the prosecution, an anonymous hate letter written to John Howard Conrad at his Denver hotel long before the trial's beginning. (Where had it been all this time, though reference was made of it during the trial?)

John Conrad:

Members of the Barnaby family will leave Providence to volunteer to take all the skeletons out of the family closet—Mrs. Conrad's! And all of them! Be on the lookout! They are *mad* at you and they will tell all that they know. Be warned and be on the watch, for they are coming. They leave Providence either Friday or Saturday night. A FRIEND. They volunteered to come to Captian Ballew [sic] for they hate you. They will try to prove that your wife tried to elope with Winship before you knew her and other very bad things!

The prosecution brought back their handwriting expert, who swore it was in the same handwriting as Graves' letters, "though very disguised."

What does that really mean? Disguised?

Graves slammed back in his chair, a grim smile of incredulity and frustration on his face. He pounded on the arm of the chair, then conferred with his lawyers. Unfortunately, this little bombshell was too well-timed: the defense's handwriting expert, the one who said the writing of the lethal label was a woman, was unavailable for refutation.

And on that anticlimactic note the testimony ended. The long trial was virtually over, except for the windy final arguments.

In his memoirs Furman remembers Graves leaning over to him and saying; "Having known Ballou all my life—would I spell his name wrong? As an army officer myself would I get his rank wrong? Would I use that primitive language?"

"Not unless a person were trying to throw them off the scent, and that's what they're implying," replied the lawyer.

As they walked out of the courtroom Tom looked gloomy. "Tell me, friend Furman, how do you realistically see my chances?" And Furman said, trying to keep up his own spirits, "Be of good cheer, Tom—remember that almost no one has been convicted on such flimsy circumstantial evidence." But Macon interjected firmly, "I see the odds as sixty to forty."

"For or against me?" asked Tom.

"Against," said Macon reluctantly.

187

The final arguments were all that remained, and the next day Judge Rising instructed the jury fairly and sensibly in this manner (and in turn-of-the-century judicial terminology):

The court instructs you that the law presumes the defendant innocent, and this presumption continues until overthrown by evidence sufficient to exclude all reasonable doubt of his guilt. The indictment against the defendant is no evidence of his guilt, but is merely a formal charge for the purpose of putting him upon trial. You ought to commence the investigation of the case with the presumption that the defendant is innocent of the crime of which he is accused, and you should act upon this presumption throughout your consideration of the evidence unless this presumption of innocence is overcome by a proof of guilt so strong, credible and conclusive as to convince your minds beyond any reasonable doubt of his guilt. Then you ought to acquit him. The rule of law, which clothes every person accused of crime with a presumption of innocence and imposes the state the burden of establishing his guilt beyond a reasonable doubt, is not intended to aid anyone, who is in fact guilty of crime, to escape, but it is a humane provision of the law, intended as far as human agencies can, to guard against the danger of an innocent person being unjustly punished.

After the windup, Justice Rising goes on:

The court instructs as a matter of law that the burden of proof is on the prosecution to establish by the evidence beyond a reasonable doubt, first, that the deceased came to her death by poison; second, that it was administered to her by the defendant, or that he caused it to be ad-

188

ministered to her in her lifetime: third, that the defendant administered, or caused to be administered, the poison to the deceased, willfully and knowingly and with the intention of depriving her of life; and fourth, that the deceased actually died from the effects of the poison so administered to her. There are material and essential propositions necessary to be established to warrant a conviction, and if you entertain any reasonable doubt upon either of them then the prosecution has failed to establish its case and you should acquit the defendant.

The court further instructs you that in considering the question whether the defendant did or did not administer or cause to be administered poison to the deceased as charged in the indictment, if you believe from the evidence beyond a reasonable doubt that defendant sent, or caused to be sent to the deceased, poison, with the intention that she should take a swallow of it, then you are authorized to find the fact that he administered such poison to the deceased.

The court instructs you that in this class of cases, where the indictment charges that death was caused by poisoning, it is not necessary to prove the particular substance or kind of poison used, nor is it necessary to give direct and positive proof of what is the quantity which would destroy life, nor is it necessary to prove that such quantity was found in the body of the deceased.

Here, in effect, Judge Rising seems to be saying that all the nitpicking about grains of cyanide and Fowler's Solution that Stevens forced Graves to endure has no bearing on the case—allowing the jury to believe, if they wish, that a trained medical man might as easily send enough poison to kill an elephant as one comely widow.

189

It is sufficient, if you are satisfied by the evidence beyond a reasonable doubt that the death was caused by poison of some kind, and that the poison was administered by the defendant, or that he caused it to be administered to the deceased with the intent of causing her death.

Judge Rising goes on to urge that the jury, when considering the case, not go beyond the evidence to hunt up doubts, nor entertain such doubts "as are merely chimerical or conjectural. A doubt, to justify an acquittal, must be reasonable and must arise from a candid and impartial investigation of all the evidence in the case, and unless it is the same kind of doubt which in the grave transactions of life would cause a reasonable and prudent man to hesitate and pause, it is insufficient to authorize a verdict of not guilty."

And this I find quite interesting for it combines schizophrenically the strengths and weaknesses of justice as administered by mortals. It brings to mind that biblical saying, "Be as wise as serpents, as innocent as children."

Hear Judge Rising proceed:

You are not at liberty to disbelieve as jurors if from the evidence you believe as men. Your oath imposes on you no obligation to doubt where no doubt would exist if no oath had been administered.

A reasonable doubt cannot be found upon any sensibility on the mind of any juror as to the consequence of his verdict. You should not create sources or materials for doubt by resorting to trivial or fanciful suppositions and remote conjectures as to the possible statement of fact differing from that established by the evidence. If, after considering all the evidence, you can say that you have an abiding conviction of the truth of the charge,

190

then you are satisfied beyond a possible doubt.

The court instructs you that the law requiring you to be satisfied of the defendant's guilt beyond a reasonable doubt in order to warrant a conviction does not require that you should be satisfied beyond a reasonable doubt of each link in the chain of circumstances relied upon to establish the defandant's guilt.

Remember how Stevens chose to link "the chain of circumstances" and to flog Graves with it. So many weak yet damaging lines of slander and insult, from Conrad and Trickey and Stevens himself, and yet Judge Rising then allows:

It is sufficient if, taking the testimony all together, you are satisfied beyond a reasonable doubt that the defendant is guilty.

The court instructs you that what is meant by circumstantial evidence in criminal cases is the proof of such facts and circumstances connected with or surrounding the commission of the crime charged as to tend to show the guilt or innocence of the party charged, and if these facts and circumstances are sufficient to satisfy you of the guilt of the defendant beyond a reasonable doubt, then such evidence is sufficient to authorize you to find the defendant guilty. In its consideration it should have its fair weight with you, and if, when it is taken as a whole, and fairly and candidly weighed, it convinces the guarded judgment a reasonable man would ordinarily make under like circumstances. The law exacts the conviction of a person charged with having committed a crime when there is legal evidence to show his guilt beyond a reasonable doubt, and circumstantial evidence is legal evidence.

191

"Circumstantial evidence." It brings to mind nightmarish possibilities. Think of the frequent newspaper accounts of the wrong man being jailed on circumstantial evidence.

> The court instructs you that where a conviction for a criminal offense is sought upon circumstantial evidence alone, the person must not only show by a preponderance of the evidence that the alleged facts and circumstances as are absolutely incompatible upon any reasonable hypothesis with the innocence of the defendant, and, when considered together incapable of explanation upon any reasonable hypothesis other than that of the guilt of the defendant; and, in this case, if all of the facts and circumstances relied on by the people to secure a conviction can be reasonably accounted for upon any theory consistent with the innocence of the defendant, or if such facts and circumstances do not satisfy you beyond a reasonable doubt of his guilt, then you should acquit him. But if you believe from the evidence beyond a reasonable doubt that the facts and circumstances given in evidence, and proved to your satisfaction in the manner stated in these instructions, are absolutely incompatible upon any reasonable hypothesis other than that of the guilt of the defendant, then such facts and circumstances are sufficient to authorize you to find the defendant guilty.

Rising emphasized that the burden of establishing a case against the defendant lies upon the prosecution. "And," he added, "even if it be conceded that somebody murdered the deceased, yet the defendant is not required to prove who committed the murder. The prosecution is required to prove beyond a reasonable doubt that the defendant, and not somebody else, committed the murder charged in the indictment."

Think back on the trial; the *only* person the prosecution went

192

James Belford
Assistant to Stevens

Dr. Graves pleads "Not guilty"

after tooth and nail was Dr. Graves. Graves was considered—or at least was portrayed by Stevens—as guilty from the start. Mrs. Worrell, Bennett and Kitty Graves were handled with kid gloves.

> It is not sufficient to justify you in a verdict of guilty that the evidence discloses that the deceased was murdered and that the defendant or somebody else murdered her, or that the probabilities are that the defendant and not somebody else murdered her. It must be shown by the prosecution beyond a reasonable doubt that the defendant is the guilty party.

All Stevens had managed to show was that Graves had a bad memory for dates and problems dealing with the press. But his badgering had weakened the doctor until, hollow-eyed and haggard, he did indeed look and act like a man tortured within.

> The court instructs that you, when the verbal admission of a person charged with a crime is offered in evidence, the whole of the admission must be taken together, as well that part which makes for the accused as that which makes against him, and if part of the statement, which is in favor of the defendant, is not disposed of, then such part of the statement is entitled to as much consideration from the jury as any other part of the state.

So much for Judge Rising's profundity.

Then came the pit bull, swaggering to center stage in front of the jury box. Stevens began by going right to the heart of the matter.

"If Thomas Thatcher Graves, with his weak, vacillating nature, did not prepare the poison which, covertly sent, accomplished the death of his benefactress and friend, who had elevated him from poverty to independence, the government cannot expect you to find him guilty."

Then Stevens said there was no doubt of the guilt of the accused—"that tramp of a doctor and adventurer and the crooked lawyer who conspired to deprive this feeble, paralytic old lady of her estate and administer deadly poison to their victim! There was never a happier home, more loving father, mother and children than the Barnabys—and the Conrads—they were together a happy family in the Adirondacks, in Providence and elsewhere, until these vultures gathered for the spoils!"

Happy? Hearing this, I recall the line from Tolstoy that all happy families are happy for the same reasons but that unhappy families are unhappy for different reasons. Stevens pounded away:

"Where did those villainous insinuations emanate from? Where did the loving message come from to Mrs. Barnaby that her husband had left one hundred thousand dollars to a mistress? From the same source that the blackmail letter of December 4, 1891, did."

Stevens then painted a portrait of the rich widow fleeing from her cruel keeper, Dr. Graves.

"There was nothing left for Mrs. Barnaby except the right to live when she went to California, owing to the omnivorous grasp of her evil-wishers. If she died, there was left a sole executor without bonds. When Mrs. Barnaby left Providence, December 17, 1890, she was the victim of an ill-designed and villainous conspiracy by two plunderers wearing ex-army buttons, and nothing was left to her executor but her life."

And so on for several hours in his inimitable style. The next day it was the defense's turn, and the audience was eager. Macon was to make the first part, followed by Furman. When he did not come in with the others at nine-thirty A.M. rumor soon spread through the benches that the elderly Macon was ill. Mrs. Graves was not present, and had not been in the courtroom since the day she testified.

Finally a pallid Macon did arrive, and was allowed to sit while he gave his address. He was weak and faint as he sat in an armchair facing the jury. His voice was scarcely audible. He began by saying that he had come at personal risk to defend a client, a duty he had to perform even if it should cause his death—it would be a "satisfaction of duty well performed." He seemed to impress the jury with "the scriptural injunction of charitableness in hesitating to condemn a person for error or crime"—a call for Christian virtue that seems touchingly outdated today.

Macon said that, while he had often prosecuted criminals, it was still his duty to see that "conviction or release was not obtainable by illegal means." He said that "civilization had advanced to such a degree that it was generally recognized that it was better that ninety-nine guilty persons should escape than that an innocent man should be punished."

He mentioned the "terrible attacks of the local press upon the accused," which had "influenced the opinions of scores of persons and made them unfit for jury service."

In reviewing the prosecution's case, he said that "he had never seen such willful and malicious misrepresentations and distortion of facts. Starting with Mary Hickey he said that the prosecution had drilled her perfectly; she had testified plausibly until cross-examination. He termed her testimony "infamous," and said that, while the government had charged that the defense was losing or concealing letters, he demanded of the government why they had not produced the letter of Mrs. Barnaby to Mrs. Hickey supposedly "cautioning her to watch Dr. Graves." The witness said she had burned it. One would naturally suppose that as an old and confidential servant—as she claimed to be—she would have treasured the letter as an heirloom and legacy to her children. "Funny coincidence, that! She kept all the other letters Mrs. Barnaby had written!"

Macon read the introduction to the first will of Mrs. Barnaby. It was owing to "these pronounced and unmistakable directions" that the personal attack had been made upon Colonel Ballou.

Macon then defended the character of the colonel. He said he had learned to respect and appreciate Ballou through intimate association with him during the past six weeks. Ballou was an honorable, high-minded, intelligent and conscientious gentleman and lawyer, he was an honor to his profession, and was proof against "such malicious and unwarranted attacks," which were not based upon any evidence in the case.

Referring to the payment of the ten thousand dollars to Ballou & Jackson by Mrs. Barnaby as a fee, Macon pointed out that the practice of lawyers was to charge in proportion to the amount secured rather than for the time employed, and that this was not an exorbitant fee.

Macon said: "I will show you, gentlemen, if I have strength left me before I close, the true inwardness of this villainous conspiracy whereby an innocent man is to be murdered in order that the wills may be destroyed and the property, valued at one hundred fifty thousand dollars, may fall into the laps of the Conrad family and Miss Maud Barnaby, and as to whether this princely waiving of such a substantial sum is genuine or manufactured. To charge a man with criminality because he displayed a spirit of gratitude shows the desperate straits to which the government is brought."

(The government? Rather "Ikey" Stevens, plus Judge Rising, plus John Howard Conrad's money.)

Macon then made a sarcastic allusion to "the happy and affectionate Barnaby family," as evidenced by the bequest of $2,500 to Mrs. Barnaby by her husband, and the fact that "during the winter of her widowhood and grief she did not stay with her affectionate and dutiful son-in-law, but went to Saratoga, California, and elsewhere. If she was quote paralytic, helpless, infirm and weak-minded unquote, why did the dutiful and affectionate son-in-law and daughter not even bother to find out the name of her physician, or make some effort to make her life peaceful, happy and contented?"

Macon, mindful that adjournment was near, described the

strained relations between mother and daughters, their separation and non-communication for four years. "How deep this alienation must have been when the mother and daughters could not lay it aside over the bier of the father!" Macon frequently stopped to gulp beef tea for strength, and by the noon recess he was making a superhuman effort to complete his address.

Furman recalls in his memoirs that over lunch at Tortoni's, he said to Graves:

"Tom, I have to warn you, Macon is not going to hold out much longer—he's a sick man and shouldn't even be in there. I'll be taking over tomorrow. Tom," I said, "we're coming to the end and I am not as confident as I was. In fact, we are in trouble. I never quite reckoned on Stevens' tactics and the power of Conrad's money. If there is anything you haven't told me now is the time to tell me before I go out there in front of the jury." Tom closed his eyes and shook his head. "Tom," I said, "I have not asked you before directly but I shall ask you now as your lawyer and friend: do you know who the murderer is?" He only looked at me and shook his head, and I saw how exhausted he was. "You cannot tell me or you will not tell me?" He sighed. "I *can* not tell you," he said.

But I know in my heart that he knew who the murderer was—and it was definitely not he himself.

"Tom," I said, "anything at all—give me anything! I cannot go out there tomorrow with nothing."

Tom answered as though in a trance: "One day I came back from a two-day business trip to New York not long before the murder, and I went to my laboratory and I noticed the recent smell of the bunsen burner; then looking around I saw a canister not quite in the right place, a bell jar here, a beaker there where it should not

197

have been. Not ransacked, you understand, just changed. I am fanatically neat and precise by nature. I *always* keep my porcelain canisters of important medicine in alphabetical order: this day 'B' preceded 'A,' totally out of the ordinary!"

I was for a moment confused and I said lightly, "Tom, do you mean 'A' as in aspirin?" And he said calmly enough, "'A' as in arsenic."

"Had the house been broken into?" I asked.

"The back door was open but not broken into. That was all."

"And Mrs. Graves?"

"Out of town," he said laconically. "For the day."

I am afraid I lost my temper with poor Tom. I hit at him with such accusations as "why didn't you tell me sooner," and so forth.

"They wouldn't have believed us," he said resignedly.

My personal belief is that after the scene Tom described he then confronted the murderer and learned the truth, and then had to practice to deceive at great effort for the few months that remained of his natural days.

I left Tom to rest quietly in the booth while I hurried over to the Vallejo Hotel. I was shown up to the suite which Mrs. Graves occupied with Tom's mother. Kitty was lying on the chaise, a blanket over her legs. The doctor was just leaving and cautioned me not to tire her or agitate her in any way. I sat next to her and as always was struck by her fragile beauty and youthful charm. She greeted me with a smile, though she was very pale and her eyes hollowed.

"Kitty," I said, "I'm going before the jury tomorrow for the last time. Is there anything you can tell me—

198

anything at all that might help Tom? We are afraid he might be convicted."

"Convict Tom?" She gave a little laugh. "Why, they wouldn't do that—they know Tom wouldn't hurt a fly. In just a few days now Tom and I will be going home back East to our rose garden, you'll see."

I assayed a few more questions but I saw she was not really hearing me, and I took her hand and told her to be of good cheer and to hope and pray for the best, and then I went back to the courtroom."

Pretty, pretty Mrs. Graves. And was not poisoning said to be a woman's art?

The afternoon session commenced at two o'clock. There was a perfect jam, and the courtroom was a scene of great animation and excitement before Judge Rising rapped his gavel!

Macon resumed his seat in his revolving chair directly in front of the jury. During the break he had been able to lie down for a few moments. His voice was now sturdier than at the morning session.

The jury might draw the inference from the fact that Mrs. Barnaby, helpless, paralytic, and mentally weak, was turned out of doors with a paltry annuity of twenty-five hundred dollars, while an estate valued at one million, seven-hundred and fifty thousand dollars was left by her husband. Under these circumstances was it not natural that when Mrs. Barnaby went to consult her friend Dr. Graves he should tell her that she must fight for her rights, and suggest to her to consult counsel? She secured Colonel Ballou, a fine lawyer, and yet District Attorney Stevens called him an adventurer, conspirator, scoundrel and co-robber.

199

Macon referred to the proposed purchase of the cottage in the Adirondacks, and asked the jury how she could have possibly purchased a $4,000 cottage on a total income of $2,500 per year? No wonder that Dr. Graves cautioned her against her extravagance with a harsh scolding letter:

> Admitting that it was of a threatening character, there was no connecting link calculated to warrant the statement that it was consistent with the doctor's guilt. The assassin theory of the government is not tenable, as contrasted with the theory of friendship and precaution. The Sallie Hanley letter was written for the protection of Mrs. Barnaby from the influence of Bennett, who wanted her to buy a house which he owned and desperately wanted to dispose of at an exorbitant figure.

Macon defended the character and reputation of Sallie Hanley, "a poor working girl":

> Had the defense been given the opportunity to prove characters, the hellhounds of the Pinkertons would have sought to defame her character and swear her out of court. They have shadowed her constantly since her arrival here, eager to blast her name and drive her out of town, but no evidence is given against her by the government witnesses. The detective force has permeated Denver until the system has become rotten, but even with this agency and Conrad's millions behind the government they have not been able to attack her purity, fidelity and integrity.

Then he really poured it on.

As the Scripture illustrates, sympathy and justice would go hand in hand, and from the bier in which the government would seek to bury the accused, this the jury can be your verdict bid him to rise and be restored to his wife and mother!

This pathetic allusion produced a feeling of deep emotion in everyone, including the lawyer who sank back in his chair and with trembling hand revived himself with sips of beef broth. Dr. Graves, his mother, and Colonel Ballou were moved to tears.

Macon went on:

As a refutation of the accusation that the doctor conspired to rob Mrs. Barnaby, the fact was in evidence that as soon as he got the eighty thousand dollars he invested it in bonds and securities of no value to himself. If he desired to rob and murder he could have sent his "gift of death," drawn the money or obtained a check on a Canadian bank, and in ten hours he could have been free from arrest and prosecution. These investments are an emphatic contradiction of the theory of guilt!

Macon called attention to an interesting fact about the reception of the package containing the bottle of poison in Worrell's office: the bottle, from the time of its shipment to the arrival in the office, had been corked seventeen days. And yet Mr. Schermerhorn took the cork stopper out of the bottle with a light twist of his fingers, notwithstanding the saturation to which it must have been subjected and which would naturally have swelled it—an indication that it had been opened recently. He also emphasized that the original wrapper around the package had been destroyed, and that another was substituted, when Worrell, Jr., took it to his house. The lawyer said if that original wrapper had been preserved it might have given a clue to the identity of the sender, and the handwriting might have been compared with the label on the bottle. Might it not be possible that the medicine Mrs. Barnaby had sent for from Dr. Graves and which had arrived about the same time, that an exchange of wrappers might have taken place in the Worrell office? This set the courtroom to whispering.

Macon, though weakening, made some other telling points:

On her deathbed Mrs. Barnaby asked young Worrell to include her very best wishes to Dr. Graves and to come to her quickly, hardly the act of a person who was hostile to another person, as the prosecution contends. Of course, the letter arrived after her death.

And about her alleged deathbed utterance: "Do you suppose Dr. Graves could have done this?" Now you get a bunch of old biddies fluttering around a sickroom and they could hear just about anything they wanted to hear and nobody to refute them!

And:

It was to the interest of the Worrells, against whom there were incriminating reports for a time and who we are aware *did* know the contents of the will, and in whose house Mrs. Barnaby died, to shift the responsibility to Dr. Graves.

In the case of Graves:

The question of motive was wanting, except in the gratuitous opinion of attorney Stevens, guessing, speculating that the doctor knew the contents of the will. Dr. Graves did *not* know and courtesy and professionalism dictated to him not to ask. As to the statement that Dr.

202

Graves was executor without bonds and could not be held personally responsible for the moneys and securities, the legatees had a remedy in the courts if they were dissatisfied with the prisoner.

Now here Macon makes a very important point:

The death of the principal—Mrs. Barnaby—would annul his power of attorney and deprive Graves of his salary, and hence no motive can be assigned for the crime. The defendant is not stupid! It comes back to why would he kill the goose that lays the golden eggs. Bilk her? Perhaps. Murder her? NEVER! If the doctor had wanted to take the money of the estate he would have resorted to some more intelligent plan.

Another overlooked point:

The fact that many letters beneficial to the doctor have been lost—or stolen—is evidence of his honesty.

Another good point:

If the doctor wanted her money he would not have invested in quote worthless securities unquote, as claimed by the state; he would have nipped off with them.

And still another score:

The statement by Mrs. Worrell that Mrs. Barnaby said in her house in Chester that quote Dr. Graves would be the ruin of her yet unquote is totally contradicted by the fact that a week later Mrs. Barnaby gave Dr. Graves the same bequest of twenty-five thousand dollars in her sec-

ond will. Conrad had a double motive in expending so
much money in prosecuting the accused—he is the sort
of man who if he feels himself wronged, will follow a
person for revenge to the grave.

Macon predicted (correctly as we shall see later) that whether
Dr. Graves was convicted or acquitted, Conrad would contest the
Chester will, in order to benefit his children.

"And may I point out again," Macon stated, "that Dr. Graves
received the same amount in both wills; so it was no matter to
him. As to the interviews in the Barnaby mansion, the point was
made that although Conrad had called into service Mr. Hanscom,
one of Pinkerton's so-called best men, when Conrad said the confession was made to him, he had ordered the quote experienced
detective of crime unquote out of the room." Macon suddenly
stopped talking, short of breath. He managed to gasp, "Thank you
gentlemen—I think...I must retire."

He was helped from the courtroom and Furman took over.
Though obviously sincere, Furman simply was not the lawyer Macon was. Where Macon went for facts, Furman leaned on rhetoric,
classical allusions and biblical stories.

He started out calm and deliberate but as he warmed up his
voice rang out in fancier tones. He indulged in elaborate gestures
and mannerisms as he denounced the conduct of the government
attorneys and the motives of the chief prosecuting witnesses. In
the middle of one biblical reference, he suddenly dropped the
stentorian tones of an orator to look at the jury box and ask: "Are
you sick, sir? Will you have water or air?"

It was directed to a juror named, ironically, Boring, who was
showing signs of distress. He replied, "I have a very severe headache and you've given it to me! We've been listening to stories for
several weeks. What we want now from you is the law and the
evidence!"

Judge Rising appeared astonished at this breach of court etiquette but said: "Kindly continue, Judge Furman." Furman looked nonplussed but recovered his poise and promised to close his argument in two hours.

Two hours—no wonder Boring was bored. But why hadn't anyone complained during the days of ruthless badgering by Stevens? Was badgering and slandering more interesting than "stories" of a man's virtues?

Furman then turned toward the jury:

Gentlemen—there is at least one subject in which we are all pleased. That is that this trial is drawing to a close. For weeks it has been a strain on all the minds engaged in it. On me it has been a tremendous burden, opposing three of the most distinguished lawyers in Colorado, backed up by one million dollars in cash and the scurrilous Pinkertons' Agency.

They say that Conrad has no object except to procure law and justice. Didn't he prove it by blubbering right here in the court? But what about never inquiring about his poor old mother-in-law of whom he was so terribly fond that he hadn't seen her or communicated with her for four years. There must be a great change of character here. The only change in sacred or profane history equal to this was that of Saul of Tarsus, and it took a light from heaven to change him. What light has broken on John Conrad? "Governor" Conrad, God save the mark! Or "Senator" Conrad—angels defend us! This man, who says his father-in-law's estate was one million, seven hundred and fifty thousand dollars, but he doesn't care about money; oh no, he didn't even look into it! He's above caring about mere money. Why, then, does he wish to crush his miners striking out in Montana if he doesn't care about money? He swore that he was not interested in the wills, because he wanted to show that he had no motive. But Stevens told him that now he ought to break those two wills! And you watch, he will! If he does he will collect all these trial costs out of that money and a whopping lot more. And he says: "But I don't care for that!"

Furman had a good head of steam up now:

They say *homo sapiens* is the only animal that bares its teeth to indicate amiability. Well, I don't know about you gentlemen, but when John Howard Conrad bares his teeth in a smile I feel more threatened than any feeling of anyone's being amiable. Course we haven't seen him smile much here, have we—he's been too busy blubbering about his poor mother-in-law. Now—Conrad says he never heard of Graves until Mrs. Barnaby's death. How can he reconcile that with his love and care for his beloved mother-in-law? Graves was her doctor—her only doctor! But you gentlemen know the name of your mother-in-law's doctor? I'll bet you do. Whether he heard of Graves or not, it is plain now that he blames Graves for making his father-in-law's estate lose one hundred and five thousand dollars, money that Conrad thinks rightfully should have gone into his pocket. No wonder he's mad at Graves for changing the original will! That's a lot of money—even to a Conrad. Conrad appealed to Dr. Graves' chivalric regard for women. He seemed to be suspicious of his own word. Will you believe a man who hardly believes himself? Conrad said, "If you will go and talk over the matter with my wife it will do her good." Did he mean that? Talk about Johnny, who sat there and boohoo-hooed! I'll tell you, those Montana people had level heads when they elected him to stay at home and not go to Washington!

206

Appreciative laughter. Furman is winning friends and points by giving "Ikey" Stevens back some of his own medicine, and "Crying Johnny," as Conrad is known on the street, is hardly popular.

Furman, now confident, goes in for the kill:

Let us look a little longer at Johnny. He says to Graves, "come over, doctor, and let us talk about the will." And yet he said in his own evidence he didn't care about the will. He used it as a bait, or as he says, he used it as an excuse for getting the doctor to talk about the bottle. If Graves had already confessed to sending the bottle, why did he need to talk about it any more? Let's hear from Johnny again—this "rugged son of justice." Johnny ought to put over his door a sign I once saw in Texas, "all kinds of twisting and turning done here." What did little Johnny say? "I told him [Graves] I felt it was necessary to publish in the papers that he'd handled the business all right"— but he said in his testimony he did not feel it necessary. But he is worth millions! What cares he for the truth? But if I were to spend the time pointing out all of Johnny's contradictions, this argument would never come to an end.

Now, let's compare Conrad's testimony and Hanscom's. Granting they are consistent in themselves, let's see whether they cross each other or not. "It was never mentioned that Graves should sign a statement," was Conrad's testimony in regard to the confession. Hanscom testifies: "I think Conrad asked him to make a statement in writing." Which was right, Johnny or Charlie? Again, Johnny testifies, "Graves said bring in Howard; I sent that bottle, and I might as well go to hell by one route as another." What did Hanscom testify? "Graves said I sent a bottle," and so forth, and then he went on to explain that the doctor did not particularize as to the

207

bottle or Mrs. Barnaby. Oh, yes, sure, let's hang Dr. Graves because Johnny blubbered!

Furman claimed that the prosecution had to "corkscrew the statements from Hanscom," which, when obtained, failed to corroborate the reckless statements of Conrad. Furman then showed that their testimony disagreed as to whether there was any quarrel between Conrad and Graves. For example, there was Conrad saying that their relations at the interviews were pleasant and harmonious, while Hanscom said that there "were loud and boisterous words."

Furman emphasized the point that if the doctor wanted to cover up his conspiracy to secure the estate he could have falsified the accounts and presented them in court. In regard to the claim that the doctor had purposely lost his account books, Furman made it clear that Conrad in his testimony had admitted that Dr. Graves had earnestly requested him to accompany Graves to his house to look over the books right then and there, but that Conrad had refused. If the doctor had been dishonest he never would have volunteered to let Conrad see them, would he?

In closing Furman said that if Dr. Graves sent that bottle he was a villain of the deepest dye; hanging was too good for him. There should be no compromise verdict. "Break his neck, or turn him loose," Furman challenged and looked the jury right in their eyes.

He told them they would render a just and honest verdict. Then, raising his hands toward heaven, he urged them "to weigh the evidence judiciously and impartially so they could stand by their decision when before Almighty God to answer for the deeds done in the body."

The Nietzchean belief that God is dead had not yet permeated America, and Furman's act, so easily mocked today, was taken seriously and respectfully.

District Attorney Stevens began his closing address at one o'clock.

Every eye rested upon him. The spectators realized that the trial was drawing to a close and that this last fiery flurry might decide everything, one way or another. His address was deemed by the morning newspaper "clear-cut and logical, and was a potent illustration of the supremacy that logic holds over *rampant rhetoric.*"

Was this aimed at Furman's biblical references? From the beginning, the Denver press seemed to be in Conrad's more than ample pocket. He had bought much of the New England press—Trickey and Lincoln as much as admitted that—so why not Denver's?

Stevens' speech took six hours and a half to complete, and began this way:

> Gentlemen—I now arise to perform a duty I would gladly see someone else assume, *not*" (a look of contempt at Graves) "because of the defendant on trial—hardly—but because of the law-abiding citizens of Colorado. We have heard a great deal about this question of quote life in the balance unquote and whether you should or should not take it.
>
> Gentlemen, you and I are sworn officers of the state. Who considered the "life in balance" of the victim? Not Dr. Graves, I'll tell you! For the good doctor the Hippocratic Oath became the hypocritic oath when he needed it. It is your duty, as it is mine, to consider not the consequences of your verdict, but to say to the people here today that their laws shall be faithfully enforced. It is not pleasant to take a life, but on the other hand duty is duty and to take a murderer's life, as he so blithely took his victim's, should not bother your conscience at all. It is for a cause we are here in this temple of justice—the institutions that we are here to uphold! What is a life compared with the prosperity of this government? In the last war thousands of lives were sacrificed to sus-

209

tain the glorious government we live under. I remember
reading an incident of the late war. One army beside the
Rappahannock played the tune "Star-Spangled Banner."
The other played "Dixie." But both joined in the tune
of "Home, Sweet Home." Well, that home for all of us
in America, and in particular for people of this courtroom, is this glorious new law-abiding state of Colorado.

(How ironic: Dr. Graves had risked his life repeatedly in the
Civil War while "Ikey" Stevens was a child, safe at home.)

It has been charged that there is a foul conspiracy to take
this murderer's life. If so, I am the chief conspirator. I
alone am responsible for this man being placed on trial.
If there is a conspiracy I must be the most infamous
murderer in the world. A great deal has been said about
the Pinkertons being engaged—I realize that not everyone is in favor of the Pinkertons and their methods. But
what difference does it make what power brings a defendant into a court for the trial for the most heinous
crime known in history? It is demagoguery! Would you
acquit him because the Pinkertons furnished some of the
evidence?

Hour after hour, Stevens rehashed the entire testimony with no
new ideas introduced.
Finally, he says abruptly:

Gentlemen, that disposes of all the matters I have time
to discuss. I think you carry a clear remembrance of all
the testimony. If you desire to be enlightened on anything, make the request and I will read to you from the
notes.
This has been a wearisome trial to all connected with

it. It is wonderful you have stood up so well and been able to pay such close attention, and I thank you for it. I can't impress upon you half the feeling I experience of the importance of this case to your friends, neighbors and the community.

Hang a man—whether or not you're convinced of his guilt—and save an insecure young cowtown's reputation: that seemed to be the real message "Ikey" Stevens left with the jury.

Fourteen

It was six-thirty P.M. when District Attorney Stevens completed his argument. Three bailiffs were sworn to guard the privacy of the jury and all fifteen left the courtroom. The jury agreed to defer consideration of the verdict until after supper and returned to their rooms at eight P.M. on the top floor of the courthouse. The deputies guarded all approaches to the rooms. During their absence, the mob which had filled the courtroom showed no inclination to leave. A bailiff had to ask a woman to put a roast beef sandwich back in her purse or leave the room. As the spectators awaited the verdict, the courtroom buzzed with pro- and anti-Graves bias. "Not guilty, I say!" was heard more often than the reverse. Two men in the back had a scuffle over Graves' guilt or lack of it and separating them the bailiff knocked—of all things—a bottle of whiskey to the floor, which shattered loudly. The scufflers were ejected.

The court had directed Deputy Coryell to take charge of the accused, since his bond had been vacated, and Dr. Graves was permitted to dine in the deputy's presence with his wife, mother and Dalzell in the elegant dining room at the Hotel Vallejo. At the table the party was cheerful and expected an acquittal or a hung jury at worst. Finally Dr. Graves leaned over to the adjoining table to ask Deputy Coryell what his opinion was.

"My honest opinion?"

"Yes, of course," said Graves.

"My true opinion is that the best you can hope for is a verdict in the second degree."

Graves was taken aback but said nothing. Kitty smiled and said brightly, "You, sir, shall be proven wrong and will owe us a bottle of champagne afterwards!"

"I hope so madam," said the deputy. "I hope so with all my heart."

After this the party grew quiet and did not discuss the matter any more.

Before dinner was through, Graves said lightly: "You all stay here—I think I'll go back to the court."

"God bless you, Tom," said Kitty as they kissed good-bye. "You have all my love always."

In the courtroom Graves seemed confident and self-possessed and chatted freely with his lawyers and friends. He said that in the event of an adverse decision "the old Puritan blood would brace him to stand the ordeal, whatever it might be."

The arrival of Dr. Graves in the courtroom was the signal for excited whispering. As he passed the curious faces, "his personal appearance was dissected and his guilt or innocence read in his countenance," a reporter noted. The doctor turned around and surveyed the big audience. A smile played upon his features. Some remarked how confident he appeared of his acquittal; others said he was feigning it, whistling in the dark.

Time wore on and the hands of the large clock against the wall pointed at nine o'clock. Still the twelve men did not return, and even the judge had not arrived. The people began to grow restless, but none left.

At nine-thirty P.M. Clerk Cobbey appeared at the courtroom door.

The verdict was in. There was great excitement in the courtroom. Impulsively, men and women stood up on the seats and on the court railing. Some were knocked to the floor as others pressed to the front to Dr. Graves' face when the verdict was read. Dr. Graves sat back in his chair nervously.

When Judge Rising entered at nine-thirty-five P.M., order was restored. He instructed the excited spectators to take their seats, which they did, no doubt in breathless expectation. The moments seemed like hours, as they waited for the appearance of the jury. A deputy entered and cleared the way. Then the sheriff appeared. The jury followed.

Their faces were solemn and set. Not one looked toward Graves. Their eyes were fixed upon the floor. A bad sign.

When the jury entered, Judge Rising studied them intensely; was the verdict perhaps already clear to him before a word was spoken? Dr. Graves, his face pale, also tried to read their thoughts.

The jury was seated. For a moment there was silence. Judge Rising turned in his chair, and facing the jury said calmly: "Gentlemen of the jury, have you agreed upon your verdict?"

"We have, your honor," the foreman of the jury replied in a steady voice. He handed a white sealed envelope to the judge.

Judge Rising opened the message, read it without any facial change and passed it to Clerk Cobbey.

"Gentlemen of the jury, listen to your verdict," Judge Rising said.

The clerk unfolded the document, stood in front of the bench and in a clear voice read: "We the jurors aforesaid, find the defendant, T. Thatcher Graves, guilty of murder in the first degree."

At the first words Dr. Graves, according to one newspaper report:

> turned his face away, as if forewarned of the verdict. He riveted his eyes on the ceiling and the pallor of his face was supplanted with a deep flush. The perspiration oozed from the pores of his skin and trickled down his face and hair. He sat as if stunned and breathless, his face alternately flushing and paling, and his strength seemed to desert him. He made a spasmodic effort to resume his self-control, but was manifestly thoroughly dazed and stupefied by the terrible and unexpected verdict... the effect of the grave declaration upon the immense gath-

215

ering was indescribable. The coterie of devoted women spectators who have sat daily near the doctor gave expression to their horror and bewilderment in moans and startled exclamations, and a number placed their handkerchiefs over their faces to conceal their emotion.

"Wrong!" Graves gasped hoarsely. "Gentlemen, you are mistaken! I swear, you are mistaken!"

Furman, surprised and unnerved, rose and announced in a husky voice that the defense moved for a new trial on exceptions. There was astonishment in the courtroom; since the prevailing feeling was that if the jury was unanimous, they would settle for the charge of second degree.

Judge Rising dismissed the jury and then ordered Deputy Sheriff George Means to escort the condemned man to a cell in the county jail.

Dr. Graves begged for a few moments in which "to breathe the air of freedom."

"There's no use to hurry, is there?" he asked. "Can't you give me a few minutes more?"

During the next fifteen minutes Dr. Graves looked sadly about the courtroom. Several friends crowded about him. He received their words of sympathy and he thanked them mechanically, without emotion. The bailiffs were hard pressed to clear the courtroom. The mass of men, women and children (yes, children) formed a double line outside the door through which the doctor and deputies had to pass on their way to the jail.

The three men left the courtroom immediately and walked across Glenarm Street to the Colfax Avenue Bridge, which they crossed, and headed down Colfax Avenue to the jail.

"Gentlemen," Graves said, as they passed Gallagher's crowded saloon, "I could do with a drink, and I invite you to join me."

Mr. Gallagher later reported that Graves seemed extraordinarily in control and calm, though "clearly exhausted, and he made some jokes—though I can't remember what they were. He insisted upon paying for all the others' drinks, though I tried to tell him it was on the house. A fine brave gentleman, I'd call him, convicted or not."

This is the not the way that the bailiff Wilson was to tell it to Stevens and the newspapers the next day. It would come out later—many months later—that Conrad had bribed Wilson, paying him $350 to tell this version of the walk to the jail:

I suggested getting into a carriage to go over to the jail in, but Dr. Graves objected. "Please let me walk," he said, "it may make me feel better. I shall not be alive tomorrow." Noticing the despairing condition of the prisoner we began to ply him with questions. We found him an easy subject. Graves yielded to the first inducement. I said to him: "Now, doctor, you have been convicted after a fair trail, and your only hope lies in making a clean breast of it, and relying on the clemency of the government."

Dr. Graves exclaimed: "I am not to blame, gentlemen. I am not to blame! Ballou was the author of the entire plot. He came to me and said that our finances were at a low ebb, we were behind with Mrs. Barnaby's account. There was only one way out of the difficulty, he said, and that was the way I adopted. Ballou planned the entire scheme!"

At that, Dr. Graves tottered, reeled and fell into my arms, and for a minute he could scarcely breathe. When I started with the doctor for the jail, he exclaimed in his mental agony, "My God, to my death!" and he moved along in a dazed and mechanical fashion. Once he said absently: "The whole twelve said guilty, did they," having been apparently hopeful that one man would refuse to convict. At the jail Dr. Graves gave way completely

217

to the awful effects of the situation. He sank down into the chair inside the iron bars like one in a faint. He cried softly and pitifully. All the terrible strain of the bitter trial at last bore him down. The dawning picture of his fate completed the wreck. Dr. Graves wept and was helpless as a child. Once in his distress he murmured: "I wish Ballou had never come out here!" When asked if he hoped for a new trial, he looked up and said, "I'll never live to have a new trial." As he sat in the jail office he was the picture of resigned and hopeless despair, and his answers were like the expressions of indifference in the midst of his shattered feelings. After his clothes had been removed and a thorough search of his garments and person had been exhausted he was taken to the condemned cell, in the west wing of which he was the first occupant. He hesitated on the threshold and asked in an indistinct voice: "Must I enter this cell?" He was told that he must, and moving slowly he sank upon his cot and turned his face to the wall. Deputy Sheriff Holland went on guard by the side of the doctor in the cell, and the preparations were made for a close and constant guard. He was quiet and undemonstrative during the night.

Most people reading this account completely believed that Wilson had told the truth.

At the fancy Windsor Hotel a large, boisterous champagne and caviar victory party was already beginning, hosted by John Howard Conrad for his thirty-eight witnesses, the three prosecuting lawyers, and their families.

At the Vallejo Hotel, Mrs. Graves and the aged mother of the convicted murderer were alone, except for two friends, in the parlor when the verdict was quietly announced to them by Furman. Graves'

Warden Smith
Of Canyon City Penitentiary

THE TRIAL OF DR. GRAVES.

NOT GUILTY!

By S. Edward Austin.

I.

Of a trial let me speak
Where a man accused did seek
In a western court his innocence to claim;
Dr. Graves he done his best
In that court held in the west
To prove no poisoned bottle from him came.
But he was *handicapped*, 'tis said,
By those who wish him dead,
And whose dollars just like water freely flow.
Yet he's innocent, you'll agree,
For as far as we can see
If guilty, they have failed to prove him so!

'Though he's standing on Death's brink,
He is innocent, many think,
And to the gallows he should never go;
Did he that bottle send
To his true and dearest friend?
Why, *if guilty, they have failed to prove him so!*

II.

There's his dear and trusting wife
Who loves him as her life,
Oh, what a cruel shame to turn her brain;
And make her raving mad
And believe her husband bad,
And place upon his brow the brand of Cain!
His poor old mother, gray,
Who waits to see the spray
That the boatman called "Grim Death" makes
with his oar;
If *she's* called before *he* dies
God might tell her of some lies
That were told upon the Denver Court House floor!

Though he's standing on Death's brink, etc.

III.

Of Judge Rising, I would say
If he's wrong, I'm sure some day
Retribution swift will fall upon his head!
Those twelve men good and true,
I will also say to you,
Dr. Graves you can't bring back when he is dead!
To Stevens, and Conrad too,
I will speak a word to you,
If innocent he is proved to be some time,
Oh, then what can *you* say
When he has passed away?
The world will hold YOU guilty of a crime.

'Though he's standing on Death's brink, etc.

PROVIDENCE, R. I., Jan. 15th, 1892.

GUILTY!

By S. Edward Austin.

I.

Oh, what a terrible crime
In that far-off western clime
Has just been proved against T. Thatcher Graves;
A bottle of poison sent
With a murderous intent,
Has placed him 'mong the criminals and the knaves!
While Prosperity's sun did beam,
To Mrs. Barnaby he did seem
To be the truest friend upon God's earth;
But when Misfortune's cloud
Upon him cast its shroud,
He thought he'd cast the die for what 'twas worth!

But twelve men, good and true,
Sat there the trial through,
And to the evidence attention gave;
And at last they did declare
He should swing up in the air,
And by the gallows win a murderer's grave!

II.

John Conrad is a man
Who does everything he can
To be honest and upright in everything;
He determined when he saw
The fate of his mother-in-law,
To justice the poisoner he'd bring!
He called unto his aid
Men who have a record made;
Judge Belford, Pence, and others soon found out.
Dr. Graves the poison sent
With criminal intent,
Of his guilt the jury never had a doubt!

For twelve men, good and true, etc.

III.

On the wrapper was a line,
"Please accept this whiskey fine
From dear friends in the woods who wish to you
A happy, glad New Year,"
And she drank it without fear,
Little dreaming that those words were far from true!
But up there in heaven above,
Where all is peace and love,
God's angels in a large book write each name
Of all those who commit a crime,
And Mrs. Barnaby, by this time,
Knows Dr. Graves did do that deed of shame!

For twelve men, good and true, etc.

NOT GUILTY!   GUILTY!

mother covered her face with her hands and her body trembled, but she did not weep.

Kitty, dry-eyed also, exclaimed, "Those foolish, foolish boys! They should have known better! Why, just today Tom sent me a large bouquet of roses—I ask you, would a murderer do that? How could they have done such a thing to my Tom!"

Furman put his arm around her shoulders and patted her as he would a small child.

Furman lamely told the reporters who were descending upon them that "Mrs. Graves has expressed confidence that her husband would secure a new trial even if the matter had to be taken to the Supreme Court."

Dr. Graves consented to an interview with Martin Day in his cell at the county jail on the evening following the verdict.

"The verdict was a complete surprise to me! I was never more surprised in my life. I was not expecting anything of the kind, and I would like to know what they based it on. I am totally innocent!"

"Doctor, do you say that this alleged confession is untrue, and if so what could have been the motive of the deputy sheriff in claiming that you made it?"

"It's obvious that it was done to reinforce the verdict in a doubting public's mind."

"The confession, then, is false?"

"Totally! Why should I make a confession when I have nothing to confess? I was warned against James Wilson during the trial and obviously Conrad got to him! His money can get him anything."

"What have you to say in regard to Colonel Ballou?"

"So far as I know Colonel Ballou had nothing to do with any wrongdoing. That is all I know and all I can say. As I know nothing about who committed the crime—

219

I certainly know nothing that could implicate Colonel Ballou."

Day next asked Graves his opinion on Colonel Ballou.

"Did you know that Colonel Ballou was going east?"

"For several days before the close of the trail Colonel Ballou had been anxious to go east to look after important business that needed his attention, one of which, incidentally, is to start an immediate lawsuit against Conrad—$100,000 for slander."

"Dr. Graves, what about this report of lost papers and books?"

Graves was firmly convinced that the Pinkertons or someone connected with the prosecution had gone through his papers.

"I had left them when I had taken them out to show them to Mr. Conrad the night he came from the Barnaby mansion to get a list of the securities. I had Colonel Ballou search for them, but they had been taken. Colonel Ballou informed me that the room in my house where I kept my accounts and books had the appearance of having been ransacked and searched by unknown parties. But then, as we know, that has been the standard policy that they have followed in this case."

"Please explain, doctor."

"As an illustration, I'll mention an incident that occurred the day of the opening of the arguments in the case. The day that Mr. Stevens made his speech Judge Furman handed me a package that contained my Harvard diploma, two receipts from Van Slyck in regard to the Barnaby estate and my documents showing my army record. This was in the forenoon and I placed them inside my overcoat pocket, folded my overcoat and placed it as usual on the platform in the rear of Judge Rising's chair. At noon I found the package gone. When I returned after the noon recess I spoke to Judge Furman about them, and the judge thought it best not to say anything about it as so much had been said about lost papers, and the prosecution would have claimed that it was a put-up job, as they did about the books of the Barnaby estate. Imagine, right there in the courtroom! Almost under the chair of the justice himself, my Harvard diploma, two receipts from Van Slyck and my army papers were stolen! Yet they talk about fair play!"

Graves continued: "It's just like what happened to those books and papers that I showed Mr. Conrad at my own house—if they had not been stolen I could have shown that jury to a red cent every single thing in regard to the management of Mrs. Barnaby's property and estate."

"Have you yet had any clue as to who stole your Harvard diploma and other papers in the Denver courtroom?"

"No," said Graves shaking his head, "no inquiries were made, but nothing could be learned. Whoever took them must have reached under the folds of my overcoat with the intention of searching my pocket. Any man highly prizes his diploma as it has a value outside of its intrinsic worth. With it was the program of the exercise of my class at Harvard, at which I delivered the valedictory, and which I suppose can't now be replaced. If this could happen in Denver in a courtroom it gives you a good idea of the way my papers and documents were stolen in Providence."

221

"Dr. Graves, suppose the worst should come, suppose you were to suffer the penalty of the law that may follow the verdict."

"I shall still say that I am innocent! If I should suffer the extreme penalty of the law my last words on the scaffold will be that I am innocent! I will go to the scaffold with the word 'innocent' upon my lips."

Dr. Graves then exclaimed with emphasis, "I do not know who sent that bottle. I tell you I know nothing about it. I know no more about it than you do. I tell you sir, I am innocent of this crime. I had no more to do with Mrs. Barnaby's death than a child. I know nothing. Before my Maker, sir, I say I am innocent!" He added, "I was expecting my wife today; but she has been sick, but may come tomorrow."

"Your mother is said to stand up well under this trouble, although seventy-five years of age."

"Yes, and I am glad of it," he said proudly. "She was a Thatcher and the Thatchers went to New England about the time or soon after the coming of the *Mayflower*. She has that old Puritan blood in her veins that withstands and keeps up. It is the same that enabled me to face this present trouble. I trust I have some of my mother's grit and courage in this ordeal."

Graves then curiously began to climb higher in his family tree:

"The Thatchers are an old New England family. There has always been a Thomas Thatcher in the family. The Reverend Thomas Thatcher, for whom I was named, was pastor of the old South Church, Boston, before or during the revolutionary war. It was about that time her father's family had important positions in New England. Yes, it would take some time to run through the list."

222

"Dr. Graves, it has been claimed that you had plenty of money with which to fight the prosecution."

"That is not true!" said Graves, smacking his palm with his fist. "My wife and I had about $2,000 saved up, which was put into the case. The rest was paid by my friends. If I had robbed the Barnaby estate as the prosecution attempted to show, and had been tried for embezzlement, there might have been some chance but, on the contrary, on the trial for my life I had but $2,000, which my wife and I had saved, and the rest was raised by friends. Had I had the money, I could have brought witnesses here to prove many a point that would have knocked out links in the evidence upon which the prosecution rested so strongly. But when it was proposed to send for that or this witness in the East or West the question would come up, who would bear the expense? My attorneys and myself were handicapped during the entire trial. I had not the money to bring witnesses this long distance to prove many a point in my favor."

"Name some one witness, doctor, that you wanted."

"Well, just as an example, if I had had the money I would have sent to California for a witness who would show that instead of Mrs. Worrell and Mrs. Barnaby being so friendly they had a terrible quarrel. They had a row in California, and that is why Mrs. Worrell came on alone."

"Dr. Graves, it has been said that you did not at first know the value of that letter that came back to you through the Dead Letter Office until it was explained to you by counsel. That it proved you couldn't have done it."

"That is true. I gave my attorney what letters I had. Judge Macon was looking them over and coming across that one, asked me about it, and I explained how it had come back to me through the Dead Letter Office. Judge

Macon told me it was very important, and said it must be kept under lock and key. He considered it an important document in my favor. You may say," added the doctor, "that Harry Royce, a brother of my wife, has started for Denver and is soon expected to arrive here. Yes, we will continue the fight in the courts. I am not discouraged and neither are my lawyers."

Here is reporter Martin Day's version of Graves' first meeting with his wife after the verdict, and it is worthy of any late Victorian soap opera:

From the hour that the announcement of the fatal verdict was made to Mrs. Graves on that memorable Saturday night, her mental condition had alarmed her venerable mother-in-law and intimate friends at Hotel Vallejo, and the attending physicians employed every agency in combatting the delirium and physical prostration which the painful tidings had brought. She besought the presence of her husband at her bedside with wistful and persistent entreaty and finally the physician, hopeful that the granting of her prayer might prove beneficial and stimulating, persuaded the court to direct the sheriff to allow the meeting. At 3:30 o'clock Tuesday afternoon a hack drawn by a pair of horses and a driver in full livery uniform drew up in front of the County Court House near the entrance to the sheriff's office. Presently, Under Sheriffs Ferguson, Fretz and Mr. Williams of Sterling, Illinois, uncle to Dr. Graves, came out, entered the vehicle and were driven to the county jail.

They were ushered in by Warden Hopkins, to whom Mr. Ferguson presented an official document bearing the seal of the court. It was an order from Judge Rising, procured at the instance of Judge Furman and Dr. Pfeiffer, and assented to by the district attorney, directing the warden to release Dr. Graves for the purpose of visiting his stricken and frantic wife in her apartments at the Vallejo. Warden Hopkins immediately carried the welcome intelligence to the prisoner, who lost no time in preparing for his temporary reunion with his suffering wife.

Graves was escorted to the carriage, the deputies refraining from the use of handcuffs, and the quartet was conveyed to the Vallejo, where they arrived shortly after four o'clock. The doctor was taken into the presence of his beloved, and he remained about an hour and a half in the sick chamber, Deputy Ferguson being present as a matter of precaution, while the others remained outside in the sitting room.

The scene was so pathetic and heart-rending that the deputy, hardened to the exhibition of human misery and misfortune, was overmastered by his emotion, and when an interview was sought with him, he remarked in a husky and broken voice: "Boys, I can't tell you anything. That meeting was too sacred to disclose to the public, or through the press." He said that when the doctor entered the chamber Mrs. Graves was tossing about restlessly on her couch raving incessantly over the absence of her dear Tom, and even pressing her hands to her head in a pitiful attempt to regain her reason, which was dethroned with the views of the fatal verdict, and has not since regained its control, except at infrequent intervals. The intensity of her mental and physical prostration was pictured in her pale and pinched features and the wild and frenzied glances from her eyes, which turned in every direction in unceasing and restless persistency. Dr. Graves imprinted a tender kiss upon her

225

fevered lips, and knelt at the bedside in speechless agony, and sobbing without restraint, he called her repeatedly by her pet name, "Kitty," smoothed her face and hair, and convulsively pressed her hand with the tenderest and most touching solicitude. Her delirium did not cease with his entrance, and with the exception of one or two lucid intervals, in which she gave him a smile of loving recognition and kissed him faintly, she did not manifest any perceptible indication of this presence or companionship.

Mother Graves came into the chamber and remained a few moments, and the meeting of parent and son was indescribably affecting. Her snow-white locks were partially concealed beneath her widow's cap, and she threw her trembling arms around the neck of her unfortunate son. She maintained her self-possession and checked her deep emotion with Spartan-like determination, and her words of counsel and hopefulness were freighted with the inspiration and enthusiasm of her supplications to her God for strength to bear the terrible burdens, which were offered day and night since her son was removed from her presence to his solitary and comfortless cell. Her faith in the innocence and ultimate deliverance of her son was constant and sublime, and she had nerved herself by prayer and determination, which commanded the heartfelt sympathy and admiration of the guests at the hotel and a wide circle of friends, who came voluntarily to the venerable woman in her hour of dire affliction.

The hours sped with relentless rapidity, and the deputy, in obedience to his instructions, was compelled to inform the doctor that he must prepare to return to his cell.

226

The parting scene between husband and wife was forlorn and touching as Dr. Graves caressed Kitty. Then mother and son embraced and the despairing doctor reentered the hack and returned to jail.

Dr. Pfeiffer, the family physician, used all his skills to save the doctor's wife. She was slightly improved by morning, she ate a little, and her mother-in-law looked after her.

But on Monday Mrs. Graves was in a state of almost uncontrollable mania. She would cry out "Tom! Tom! Tom is coming home tonight, and when he comes he will pat me on the head and say what has my little Kitty been doing while I was away? and I will get his dressing gown and slippers for him and he will stay with me. Won't it be nice to have Tom back." Then, in her fever, she would shout, "Where is Mr. Stevens? I must see Mr. Stevens. He took my good head away from me. I had a good head once. Where is my good head. There it is, on the pillow by Tom; but I can't find it, for I can't find Tom. I must tell Mr. Stevens how he has lied about my innocent Tom." She continued her pathetic outbursts frequently, then became silent from sheer exhaustion. An attack of the grippe further weakened her condition. Her father and brother were summoned.

Dr. Graves passed a quiet night after his painful meeting with his wife. He ate a hearty supper, was cheerful and self-possessed. He seemed resigned to his confinement in the jail. He read the papers and magazines, and for exercise walked about the corridor in front of his cell. He is reported to have said to a friend:

> If I should be hanged I want my body buried in Colorado. Leave it here until my innocence shall be known. Then I want them to take my remains back to our family burying ground in New England, but not until then. This mystery will be cleared up some time, but I do not want my remains taken home until my innocence is established, as I know it will be some day.

227

Fifteen

The death penalty was handed down on January 11 by Judge Rising. Long before the court opened the corridors were blocked, the crowd surging to the stairs and overflowing the chamber. Dr. Graves appeared promptly at ten o'clock accompanied by his counsel, his face alternately flushed and pale. Hundreds of eyes were riveted on him. The thump of a gavel brought order to the excited courtroom. Judge Rising immediately gave his decision on the motion in arrest and judgment. "I have examined the authorities; I hardly think they support the position assumed by the defense."

The judge cited Iowa authorities. He found that the questions had been ruled against as early as in the first Colorado records. He held that the first count in the indictment was sufficient. The other counts, he ruled, were also good. The words "felonious, malice aforethought" are included in deliberation of the crime and with intent to kill, and had been so ruled by the Supreme Court. The motion for an arrest of judgment was therefore denied.

Dr. Graves was then ordered to stand up to receive the death sentence. Judge Rising asked solemnly, "Have you anything to say why sentence should not be passed upon you?"

Doctor Graves, erect, replied calmly, "Your honor, I did not, in any manner, thought or deed, have anything to do with the death of Mrs. Barnaby. I never confessed that I sent that bottle, because I never sent it!"

"You may proceed, your honor. That is all we have to say," said Furman.

Judge Rising then read the verdict:

I now remand you over to the custody of the sheriff of Arapahoe county, who shall within twenty-four hours after receiving these instructions cause you to be taken to the state penitentiary at Canyon City and handed over to the warden, and on some day at some hour to be designated by that official in the week commencing on the thirty-first of January, you shall be taken to the proper place within the walls of the penitentiary and shall be hanged by your neck until you shall be dead.

Dr. Graves' face turned livid as Judge Rising pronounced the sentence. He clasped his hands tightly. There was not a sound in the courtroom. Every eye was on Dr. Graves, who stood silent, irresolute, then turned and walked steadily to his chair, and slumped into it, exhausted. His arm dropped heavily on the table, and he stared vacantly at the wall, stunned.

After leaving the courtroom Dr. Graves was returned to the condemned cell in the county jail, where he remained until the deputy came to escort him to the carriage which took him to the station. There he awaited the train for a one-way trip to eternity.

Dr. Graves spent the time walking up and down the platform, his hands clasped behind him. Besides Deputy Sheriff Smith he was accompanied by Under Sheriff Ferguson, Henry Royce, his brother-in-law, and several friends, including Dalzell. Furman was at the depot and tried to cheer him up. Dr. Graves climbed briskly on board at the platform between the smoking car and the first passenger coach.

The moment he was seated he was surrounded by friends—old and new; they leaned over the backs of the seats and sat on the arms and patted his back. The train stopped several minutes at Burnham. Those who were to leave at that point pushed to the front and offered words of good cheer. The doctor took it all almost impassively. His hat was pulled a little farther than usual over his eyes but, apart from that and from the watchful glances of the officers, there was nothing about him to indicate that he was not going on a pleasure excursion. There was much more feeling in the voices of those who spoke to him than in his own. He seemed fortified against all emotion; his replies were easy and calm.

Once, in answer to a question if there was anything he wanted, he replied, "Oh, I feel very well, very well; never felt in better health in my life." Then he added: "And I assure you gentlemen, if I am going to die I shall try to die like a man."

He would repeat this statement many times in the next months, which makes his unusual death all the more interesting...and suspicious.

The train was forty-five minutes late at Palmer Lake, where a five-minute stop was made for lunch. Dr. Graves walked briskly up the platform to the lunchroom, where he ordered a cup of coffee and a pastry, "at the same time shooting off jokes in apparently the happiest mood imaginable," as a newspaper report said. He led the way back to the car, gesturing appreciatively toward the beautiful hills less than a mile away. The lake, the mountains and the ground were covered "with spotless snow which shone like polished silver in the moonbeams." Half a dozen people had gathered at the depot to catch a glimpse of him. They said the sentiment of all the towns and villages was that the verdict was wrong; and that the sentence was too severe. Petitions were being circulated everywhere asking for a commutation to life imprisonment, a new trial, or a not guilty verdict. It all sounded like empty, wishful talk.

At the penitentiary Dr. Graves was taken directly to the death house after he had signed the death warrant in the warden's office. He was put in the second cell from the entrance next to the one occupied by a convict known as "Murderer Mora," who had done in three victims with his "skillful stiletto." When he asked who was in the cell next to him, Graves was told that it was "a man awaiting the hangman's pleasure." Past the guard, across the corridor, the door opened into the death chamber, not more than five feet away.

This was the terrible house of execution, the place where all

231

men convicted of murder in the first degree had to sit and await the noose, not knowing what day or what hour the hangman would knock at his cell door and say, "Prisoner, let's go!" Ten minutes from that knock he would be a dead man.

Every day three men would pass the cell in which Graves was confined and enter the death chamber. He knew, of course, what they did there in that mysterious room; they were testing the automatic machinery to see that all was in readiness for the day when the warden would carry out the orders of the court. From his cell Graves could hear the heavy weight as it crashed down into the well. Day and night a bag of sand weighing one hundred and fifty pounds was hung on the rope, keeping it tight and guarding against any shrinkage.

Warden Smith was, coincidentally, a good friend of Conrad's. Speaking of the advantages of the death machine, Smith jovially told reporters:

> There is no question about the safety of the instrument we use. You must understand that there are two chances for breaking a man's neck. Where a man is dropped from a scaffold he may turn or move his neck, the rope may slip and the man strangle. This is cruel. Now our system is swift, sure and painless. In the first place, a guard keeps his finger on the knot to guard against its slipping. When the jerk comes the rope tightens, and the knot tied under the left ear throws the head to one side and breaks the neck at the first joint in the spinal column, that is, by the first jerk. The falling of the weight snaps the body upward about four feet. The body falls back three feet, and there is the second chance to kill him. If, when Dr. Graves steps upon the platform, which sets the automatic machinery in motion, if it should catch anywhere, it makes no difference, for a nod from me will be noticed by a man concealed in the back room, who

232

looks through a slit in the wall, and that unnamed man
would then immediately trip the lever that would set all
the fatal machinery in motion. After the condemned man
steps upon the board and by his own weight starts the
unique system to working, the minister has just time to
repeat the Lord's Prayer. And, boys, that's it—perma-
nent!

One morning Graves sent for the warden. He complained that
his cell was too narrow and small; he did not have enough room
to exercise in. "Why, I cannot even walk in it," he exclaimed.

The warden rejoined: "Under the explicit order of the court,
Dr. Graves, you are sentenced to solitary confinement pending
your execution. I have long since been taught to obey the order
of the court."

And then Graves said, with unintentional humor, since it was a
bit late in the day to worry about that: "This close confinement is
ruining my health!"

"I will send the physician to you."

Dr. Graves shrugged as the warden went out the door and into
the prison yard.

Public opinion throughout Colorado after the death penalty was
pronounced seemed to turn sympathetically to Graves. This was
especially true in the mining regions and mountain districts. Petitions were circulated to bring pressure on Governor Routt to
commute the sentence to life imprisonment. Dr. Graves' counsel
prepared briefs to submit to the Supreme Court on the motion for
a new trial, friends of the condemned man supplied the money
and a vigorous effort was made to collect new evidence in San
Francisco and other places, to be used if a new trial was granted.
One sensational report of newly discovered evidence declared that
"a Denver detective had procured affidavits from thirty persons in
San Francisco, insinuating that Mrs. Worrell, Sr., had purchased
poison while stopping at hotels in that city with Mrs. Barnaby, and

233

had made the statement that she wished Mrs. Barnaby would die, as she was a great trouble and the only reason she remained with her was because she hoped to be remembered in her will."

Another news story, stating that a drunken man had confessed in a Denver saloon that he had sent the poisoned liquid to Mrs. Barnaby, created some excitement. Mora, the condemned stiletto murderer, was granted a stay of execution on January 18, the week in which he was to have been hanged. The news of the Supreme Court action was wired to Mora, who shouted it at Graves' cell, and the two convicts rejoiced. Graves took it as a good omen that now he would have his chance before the Colorado Supreme Court; he was not, at least, a multiple knife murderer.

Still another pro-Graves happening: A boardinghouse keeper declared that one of the jurors in the trial of Dr. Graves had, previous to being empaneled, made the statement in the presence of several people that the accused "was guilty and ought to be hanged."

The bill of exceptions in the Graves case was presented to Judge Rising by Furman on Friday, January 22. The court gave the attorney a receipt to protect the right of the cause. An order of notice was subsequently served on the prosecution, and the preliminaries observed pending the submission of the matter to the Supreme Court and the procuring of a writ of *supersedeas*, or stay of execution.

On Friday, January 29, the Supreme Court granted a writ of error, to operate as a *supersedeas*. Dr. Graves' execution was thus stayed until a further order of the court. One can only imagine the effect of this on Dr. Graves.

Following the instructions he had received in the Mora case, and under the same order, Warden Smith transferred Dr. Graves from the execution house to the cell house, where the female prisoners were confined. The condemned man would continue to receive the same treatment as before, would be allowed to wear the same clothing, and his confinement, instead of being "solitary," was now changed to "close." Dr. Graves could exercise in the corridor and choose his own food.

On Wednesday, February 3, Graves was informed that the will of Mrs. Barnaby, executed in January 7, 1891, at the Worrells' house in Chester, Pennsylvania, was admitted to probate in the Providence Municipal Court (counsel for E. S. Worrell, Sr. asked for the removal of Dr. Graves as executor and the appointment of an administrator).

Mrs. Graves and two friends went to the penitentiary on February 10 to visit her husband. She had not yet been informed that he had been sentenced to death. Pale and nervous, she was escorted from the Pullman car on the arms of her brother and the owner of the Vallejo Hotel. She was almost carried from the train and was lifted into a waiting carriage. A doctor, who examined her at the Canyon City hotel, reported that she was very feeble and showed the effects of intense suffering. Graves waited for her with "feverish anxiety."

The prison physician, Dr. Dawson, conducted Dr. Graves to the warden's office. According to a report, the meeting was a sad one. "Men trained to such scenes left the warden's office with tears in their eyes and took a walk in the cool night air to nerve them to reenter the room. They talked for an hour, these two people whose names have been in the mouth of everybody in the country for the past four months. Finally they parted, she to return to her hotel and he to the steel cage surrounded by brilliant incandescent lamps in the north wing of the main prison. As Mrs. Graves passed out of the front door she looked back and saw the heavy steel gate swinging slowly open and her husband blew a kiss of goodnight."

Meanwhile, just as Graves' lawyers had predicted in court, Conrad, with Graves out of the way, was busy breaking Mrs. Barnaby's will; with all his millions he still wanted that money. He filed an appeal in the Supreme Court, citing as the reasons for contest the allegations that Mrs. Barnaby at the time the instrument was executed was *unduly influenced by the Worrells,* and that her mental and physical condition rendered her incapable of making a will. These allegations had been substantiated during the trial of Dr. Graves for the "murder of the testatrix, and it was anticipated that the Supreme Court would set aside the will after the presentation of that and additional testimony."

Interesting little detail here. Conrad nailed Graves, but now he seems to want to get the Worrells—his "friends"—and certainly their ten thousand dollars.

As for Ballou's suit against Conrad for calling him a murderer, a small item in the paper told of the highly predictable outcome of that quixotic endeavor: "The libel suit brought by Col. Daniel R. Ballou of Providence against Mr. Conrad in the sum of $100,000, should have been entered in the Supreme Court on or before March 23, but the complainant did not comply with the forms of law, and it was said that he had decided to relinquish the suit."

This latter day David was no fool—he ultimately came to understand that Goliath had all the weapons and that a slingshot wouldn't quite do the trick.

The last month of Dr. Graves' confinement in the penitentiary was uneventful. The few who saw him never spoke to him about his case, and his only conversations were with his attorneys. He received more mail than any other prisoner in the institution—most of it, however, never reached him. The letters were mostly from sympathetic strangers addressed to his wife and mother.

Graves was never allowed to see newspapers, but he was at the end able to receive magazines and books which were sent to him. He used the prison library regularly, his last withdrawal was Vincent's *Twenty Months of Quest and Query* and Victor Hugo's *Les Miserables*.

By now his beard and whiskers had turned white and he had grown very pale; the sunshine never reached him. An impression of his situation at the time:

His cell is four and one-half feet wide and eight feet long, with a low ceiling from which is hung an electric light. A wooden bench upon which a straw tick and pillow are placed with two sheets and a blanket serves for his bed. The only other articles of furniture are a wooden chair, small stand, a small wooden bench, upon which his meals are spread, and two buckets. He does not use the allowance of tobacco that is dealt out to convicts, and one walking through the cell house early in the evening can see the men smoking pipes and reading by their oil lights behind nearly every barred door, but cell 20 is usually in darkness by eight o'clock, and its occupant is rolled in his blanket and asleep.

While Graves paces the corridor during the day, or sits at his little table in his cell writing letters or reading, he is clothed in a light wool shirt, plaid tennis jacket, gray pantaloons and slippers. As he pauses in his walk back and forth through the corridor he sees through the grated window half a hundred convicts toiling in the stoneyard, and blue coats moving about, their owners carrying double-barreled shotguns, which are at all times ready for action. Immediately back of the high stone wall of the yard the mountains loom up to a tremendous height, making a more pleasing picture to gaze upon. The walls of other buildings obscure the prisoner's view of the entrance to the Grand Canyon, from which Canyon City derives its name, and which commences within a half mile of the penitentiary.

The only work that Dr. Graves must do is to keep his cell in order. He is required to take a bath once a week, he must be in bed at nine o'clock every night, at which time the electric lights in the cells are turned off, and he is not allowed to get up until the whistle blows at 5:45 in the morning. He is not permitted to exchange a word with a fellow-prisoner if he so desired, and the only persons with whom he speaks are the chaplain and his guards.

The only visitor he has been allowed to see is his wife, who spent three days in Canyon City before her return to the East. During this short stay she called twice a day at the penitentiary and her husband was brought to the warden's office to receive her at each call, which lasted from half an hour to an hour. These visits were made in the presence of a guard and the officials of the prison were lenient in reference to them on account of Mrs. Graves' poor health. She is now recovering rapidly, has every care and attention she could desire at her brother's palatial home, and is expected back to Colorado soon. Mrs. Graves, Sr., the mother, never saw her son after the jury brought in a verdict of his guilt, as she immediately left for Hartford, Connecticut.

Many believe that a new trial will mean freedom for the accused, said the Rocky Mountains *News,* "because of the witnesses living so far away and the great expense of such a trial. The prosecution could never be conducted as thoroughly as it was before. If a new trial is refused it is thoroughly believed that he will soon suffer the death penalty, for the governor's friends and those who know him best are not slow in giving their opinion that he will never interfere in the case.

"Ikey" Stevens, in commenting upon the possibility of a new trial, declared:

Our Supreme Court is composed of most excellent and able judges. The result of a new trial in this case would be the absolute discharge of the defendant. It would be impossible to ever prosecute the case again. The wit-

238

nesses all live beyond the jurisdiction of our courts, and it was with the greatest difficulty and at very heavy expense that their attendance was secured at the last trial. It would be impossible to get them a second time to leave their business to volunteer, as we have no means of forcing their attendance.

(Money talks, nobody walks.)

Mr. Conrad informs me that he thinks that himself and family have fully discharged their duty to the good people of Colorado, and that he will never again interest himself in the matter if a second trial is ordered. If this conviction cannot be sustained, in my judgment no conviction for murder in the state of Colorado can be sustained, for the case on the part of the prosecution was one of the strongest criminal cases ever taken into a court of justice, and it was most carefully tried by the presiding judge. The result of the Graves trial has considerably raised Colorado in the eyes of the world as a law-abiding and law-enforcing community, and if it should transpire that Graves should now be turned loose, unpunished for his heinous crime, then, indeed, the state would deserve the reputation which he thought it bore at the time he sent this bottle—namely, that of being the safest place in the United States for the commission of murder.

So what was the fate of Dr. Graves? Did he get a new trial— or was he hanged?
Enter the last twist of this most bizarre murder case.

The Summing Up

The legalities dragged on and on, but finally Graves' lawyers managed to get the first verdict set aside on technicalities and a new trial was in the making.

Graves occupied himself in his cell writing letters to his lawyers and working on a book, *In the Shadow of the Gallows*, while awaiting his second trial. Although allowed special privileges, it was a long wait—he was in jail from January 1, 1892, until September 2, 1893.

On that particular—and final—day, he seemed especially cheerful. He enjoyed a hearty lunch with his wife, who had recovered somewhat from her breakdown. She came to see him every day. He joked frequently and seemed to be very optimistic and the Graveses joined one of the guards and his wife for a good meal. Dr. Graves reported enthusiastically that his lawyers had found two reliable witnesses who would testify that they saw Conrad pay $350 to Bailiff Wilson the very night he claimed that Graves had confessed after the guilty verdict. There were also several other bits of new and vital evidence from San Francisco, he said. The guard seemed unusually interested in all the new evidence and asked many questions.

Graves was in a light-hearted and joking mood the rest of the afternoon and he and his wife, according to a guard, acted "like young lovers."

When they parted at six P.M., Dr. Graves said, "Good-bye, darling—promise you'll come back early tomorrow morning!"

Graves stayed up unusually late that night writing in his cell.

241

He was last seen walking up and down the corridor with a glass in his hand.

At nine o'clock the next morning, when he failed to report for breakfast, a guard entered his cell. Graves appeared to be sleeping normally, but when the jailer shook him he saw that the doctor was dead.

What a sensation for the press. They had a field day. According to the newspapers it was clearly suicide—Graves had been able to "accumulate enough fly paper from the ceiling of his cell to soak it in water until he had a lethal dose of the poison." There was no other logical explanation.

Arsenic in the form of flypaper was said to have been administered by the twenty-six-year-old Florence Maybrick, daughter of an Alabama banker, to her fifty-year-old English husband when he died in 1889. Certainly Florence bought an extraordinary amount of flypaper just before her husband's death and certainly she was seen soaking the papers in water, but then arsenic was at that time popularly used as a cosmetic and perhaps she really did intend it for that purpose. (She was found guilty.)

Frederick Seddon, an insurance agent, in 1911 poisoned his female lodger who had signed over an annuity to him, using flypaper dissolved in water.

But flypaper did *not* cause Dr. Graves' death. He obviously did not die from arsenic; death by that poison is agony—we remember Mrs. Barnaby's lingering death, six days of screaming pain. The newspapers remarked on Graves' "placid, uncontorted features as he lay on his bed as though in peaceful sleep." Hardly the way a victim of arsenic looks when he dies. He thrashes, he screams, he tears at his throat and stomach. Yet the prison officials also backed up the flypaper theory!

What poison, then, was used and how was it obtained? Certainly Mrs. Graves wouldn't have furnished it, nor would a guard jeopardize his job by giving it to him. Visitors were carefully shaken

242

down; guards were held accountable and threatened with extreme penalties.

Another mystery in the case. Was it suicide?

Dr. Graves left several letters. In one he said cryptically: "I am afraid for my life—and I do not mean by hanging." One was to his wife—dated back in August—a twelve-page letter which was not made public. One was addressed to the people of Colorado, excoriating the district attorney and stating that the trial had cost Graves all that he and his wife owned in the world, the only way he could ensure that his wife and mother would be taken care of financially was for him to "take this way out"—they would then get Mrs. Barnaby's inheritance. He ended the letter:

> Upon my solemn Masonic oath I, T. Thatcher Graves, did not have anything to do in any way, shape, manner nor deed with the death of Mrs. Barnaby—I write this knowing what the future will soon have in store for me.
>
> The People will believe, pity, and sympathize with me. They will know that even the strongest man can be beaten down by a cyclone of filth, mud and persecution.
>
> I leave little Ikey Stevens to the people of Colorado. Please take care of him!
>
> T. Thatcher Graves
Harvard '71

To the coroner he wrote:

> Please do not hold any autopsy upon my remains. The cause of death may be rendered as follows: "Died from persecution—worn out—exhausted.

There was much speculation as to what made him do it that particular day. One theory is that the evening newspaper carried

a story that "Ikey" Stevens had announced that Conrad had discovered a teenager in Boston who swore that a man resembling
Graves had come up to him in the railroad station two years before
and paid him twenty-five cents to write the label on the fatal bottle.

(If true, then how does one explain Stevens' handwriting experts
who testified that it was Graves' writing? Or even Graves' writing,
"heavily disguised," as was claimed? Or for that matter, those who
swore steadfastly that it was the handwriting of a woman?)

Although Graves was forbidden newspapers, he might have been
told the news by a guard, then realized that he could never win
in another trial against Conrad.

Possible, but improbable.

Graves' "suicide" stirred up interest once again in the case.

Many people still believed that Graves was innocent, or at least
that his guilt had not been proven in the trial, and several editorials
were written in responsible newspapers condemning the verdict.
I am inclined to agree with them.

It was such an imprecise, sloppy way of going about the job of
extermination. If Graves were bent on murdering his benefactress,
would he not have done it in a more skillful manner? She was due
back in Providence in a week—would he not have waited and then
introduced a subtler form of poison into her body during one of
her weekly treatment sessions? Why not ever-increasing doses of
morphine? They knew about air bubbles in a vein in those days.
A man with his training, his coolness and his position as Mrs.
Barnaby's physician could surely devise some means that would
defy detection, especially since he would be the most likely person
to sign her death certificate. He, of course, knew that arsenic is
detectable in a corpse even after many years. He also knew that
two grains of arsenic will kill a person and that there was no need
to put over a hundred grains in the fatal bottle. And: would he not
have had the ingenuity to at least send an actual whiskey bottle
with liquor in it rather than a meat extract bottle filled with water?
And was he such an arch-fiend that in the wild desire to eliminate

244

Mrs. Barnaby he would risk destroying several other people who might have drunk the lethal container in the Worrell household?

And Happy New Year in *April*? A Harvard man?

Graves was certainly vacillating, inadequate and evasive on the stand. Truth has a certain ring and rhythm to it that you can't define but that you believe when you hear it. Graves' testimony about his trip west sounds phony. He might well have been less than the facade he presented to the world; he might have been a womanizer—he might have taken advantage of Mrs. Barnaby— he quite probably did—he might even have misused some of the money she had entrusted to him—though it was never proven. But a murderer?

I don't believe it.

Why has this unsolved case—and it must be considered unsolved, since the first verdict was set aside—nagged at me for some years?

As Cyril Connolly wrote about the compulsion to solve unsolved murder cases:

> Does it appeal to our vanity, the notion that logic or intuition or knowledge of the human heart can jump to the conclusion which has escaped all the experts and baffled the police? Or is it the fear that injustice has been done and the wrong person convicted? Or that a murderer may still be at large? I believe those old teamsters, vanity and curiosity, play the strongest part, and that we all feel we can complete these jigsaws with human pieces.

This is from Connolly's and James Fox's *White Mischief*, a fascinating study of an "unsolved" murder in Kenya, the Lord Errol case. But they had to go back only to 1941! How I envy them still having a host of survivors to interview. Since we're dealing here with events in the early 1890s, I have had to depend solely on letters, memoirs and periodicals for my detective work.

245

All right, then: if Graves didn't do it, who did?

I don't believe Bennett the guide did it, even though he desperately needed the $10,000; he wasn't very bright and he was a drunk, but living in the woods as he did, would he say "from your friend in the woods" on the poisoned bottle? There's a phrase in Spanish that says "Not even a drunk puts a hot coal in his mouth." *(No hay borracho que coma lumbre.)*

Since poisoning has been "traditionally a woman's art," one looks briefly at Sallie Hanley; but her motive—peevish revenge—does not appear to be strong enough. In cahoots with someone else— and tough enough to carry it off—possibly. And, remember she was "depraved" enough, having ridden a horse in the Adirondacks "astride, just like a man." But...

Mrs. Worrell, who we know not only needed the legacy but who had recently violently quarreled with Mrs. Barnaby in Santa Barbara and San Francisco (over a "vile lover"?) is a more likely candidate. Yet if she—or her son—doctored the bottle after it arrived in Denver, as the defense implied, the question still must be answered: who sent the bottle from the East in the first place? *Mr.* Worrell?

No, I don't believe any of those suspects did it. Who might have done it becomes clearer when we attend to a recently discovered letter in Des Moines; it is Dalzell writing to his brother (whose life, remember, Graves saved during a battle in the Civil War). This letter was sent one month after Graves' suicide.

> Dear Brother James:
>
> Your letter received and in hand. Sorry to hear about Cousin Martha and Newton. Insurance?
>
> Of course you are right about Tom Graves—it was a courageous act he did, not a cowardly one, done solely to insure his wife and mother's well fare [sic]. As you know, Jim, from the battlefield days, Tom met most adversity head on and with no lack of valor.

246

Rightly or wrongly, I have felt no obligation to keep my word of honor, Tom being dead, of silence about that certain important matter. In fact I felt a need to share the secret with someone connected with the case, so I contacted Lawyer Furman last week and met with him at Tortoni's.

I told him the whole story as Tom had told it to me. He listened but did not say anything about that. He didn't seem very surprised. My guess is that Tom had already told him, but like me, swore him to secrecy. Perhaps Furman felt the case was theirs anyway—won— no need to bother dragging some married woman's name in and all. Anyway, as you know, Tom never overlooked a pretty lady—they certainly never overlooked him— but Kitty was the only real love of his life and he didn't want her to be knowing about any other woman at this time.

Anyways, Furman's a good man and was fond of Tom and felt really bad about the outcome. Felt it was his fault. I asked him how. He said he should have put Kitty on "the grill," as they say.

Tom wouldn't let him do it. She won't be able to take it, is what Furman said Tom said. So he didn't ask any of the questions he would have liked to have asked Kitty.

I asked him what he would have liked to have asked her. And he said "only lots of things," had he been free to. And I saw he didn't want to talk about it anymore. And so I just asked him one simple question: where was Kitty Graves on the day the fatal package was mailed from Boston?

He smiled significantly and replied, "Boston."

Why didn't Stevens and Conrad bring that out, I asked.

"They wanted Graves," he said. "Conrad and Stevens

wanted him bad. Kitty wouldn't do." My God, I said, you don't think Kitty did it, do you?

And he said, "You heard the handwriting expert—the best handwriting expert available today—testify that a woman wrote that label. And she knew how to make poison."

That's all he would say. I was shaken. Could it be possible, gentle Kitty? Yes, I suppose it could when one thinks about her instability and all.

I'll be getting out your way around January and look forward to seeing you and Mildred after so long a time.

Yr. loving brother

Could it be possible, indeed.

Was it the work of Kitty Graves, a jealous woman, a beautiful but insecure middle-class woman, who was tired of rich Mrs. Barnaby's usurping her husband's time, attention and, perhaps in her demented mind, his affection?

Did pretty Kitty Graves, the unstable and neurotic younger woman who had first met Graves when he treated her for "nervous disorders," blow up after one of Mrs. Barnaby's childish and capricious excesses, whims or threats to get another business manager? She might have intercepted a particular letter which she took to be intimate, or a telephone message. She could have impulsively grabbed the meat extract bottle from her kitchen cupboard, emptied it and filled it with the poison mixture from her husband's laboratory (after all, she used to help him make his formula medicines). She added no whiskey, since they weren't accustomed to drinking it or having it in the house. Buying it at the corner store was too conspicuous in those days; she would take her chance that Mrs. Barnaby would take a swallow before realizing her mistake. Did she then paste on a label and, this being December, write the message "Happy New Year" and, all too obviously casting suspicion on the Bennetts, add "from your friend in the woods"? Then did something happen—did she have qualms and temporarily change her mind or, more likely, did Mrs. Barnaby, never dependable, change her travel plans abruptly? Did Kitty, when she knew that her victim would definitely be in Denver in April, then apply the telltale Providence stamps, take the train to Boston and mail the fatal package?

I'm not sure this hypothesis holds water, but it makes a lot of sense in many ways. On the other hand, while mentally unbalanced, did this childlike, fey creature have the will and guile to pull off such a crime? Furman seemed to think so.

If so, that would make Graves a noble martyr, taking the ultimate rap for his deranged wife. This might explain some of his agitation and confusion and evasions on the stand. He was a proven and authentic hero on the Civil War battlefields; was this, too, another heroic act?

I am surprised, with all the innuendo and conjecture the newspapers indulged in, that no one ever cast suspicion on Kitty Graves, not even ask where she was the day the bottle was mailed.

Ironically, since Graves' first trial was invalidated and the second never occurred, he was not legally a murderer, and Kitty Graves inherited Mrs. Barnaby's $25,000. Imagine what that sum represented in those days. It was said that she moved away from Providence shortly after being released from a mental institution and was never heard from again.

And so ends the saga of the Barnaby murder.

Or does it?

In my mother's trunk last year, as mentioned in the prologue, I found a dramatic document:

In 1908, one Wilson P. Rush, a self-styled "reporter from the Rocky Mountain *News*," claimed he interviewed lawyer Macon over several brandies at his home at Colorado Springs. The lawyer, who was so sick during the famous trial, and had had to deliver his final remarks seated, was now a hearty seventy-seven. The reporter wanted to do a magazine article on the seventeen-year-old murder and after several routine questions he asked bluntly: "Was Graves guilty?"

The old man shook his head and took a sip of brandy.

"Tom didn't do it."

"Who then, sir? Kitty? Judge Furman hints that it was Kitty."

"Possible, but if you'd known her—rather unlikely. Not sure she had enough resolve or concentration for it."

"Who then, sir?"

"There's no doubt in my mind who did it."

"Who, sir?"

"Who had the three ingredients that are necessary for any crime—motive, ability and opportunity?"

"I don't know," said the reporter. "Who?"

"Well, I've never told anyone before, but I'm getting old and I better tell someone. It was John Howard Conrad." He repeated the name emphatically. "Despite all that sobbing he did over Mrs. Barnaby's death, he hated her guts for virtually cutting his family out of the will and for embarrassing him and his political campaigns with her antics. Called her the 'She dragon.' There was only one person that he hated more—and that was her friend Doctor Graves, whom he blamed for breaking the original will. Conrad never forgave anyone who had ever crossed him—and he was out for revenge—in this case, double revenge."

"But how did he send the bottle, why did he . . ."

But the old lawyer waved his hand and said, "My boy, with his kind of money, you can do anything. For example, I don't believe Tom Graves killed himself. Not the type. Flypaper, poppycock! Tom was too smart to kill himself or anyone else with arsenic which is flypaper.

Curious, isn't it, that there was never any official announcement made about the poison used. Curious, too, that there was no autopsy... No autopsy, hear me? Illegal! Total cover-up by the warden! They got Tom into a pine box and shipped him out of the state to his family cemetery plot in the East so quick you couldn't believe it. Here I am, his lawyer, and I never even got a chance to see the body!"

"If he didn't kill himself, who did?"

"I think Conrad knew that Furman and I had a lot of new evidence—good, solid evidence. Like Conrad's bribing the bailiff to say Tom confessed, the fact that Henry Trickey was remanded to jail in the Lizzie Borden case a year later for perjury and fled the country. That the Pinkerton man Hanscom was later proved a total crook, that the detective McHenry was also a crook, and so forth. Conrad knew this, knew that we were going to win our case and get Tom acquitted. Then Conrad knew that after that, we'd go looking for the *real* murderer, and he couldn't chance that we would discover the true culprit. So what better way to kill two birds with one stone? He bribes maybe a guard, but probably his friend the warden himself, to slip a powerful, subtle poison— not arsenic—into Tom's dinner."

"But the notes?"

"The one about the suicide? Forged. The other to his wife—well, he said he was afraid for his life—and it was dated a month earlier 'in case of death.'"

It was never published—editors were afraid of slander, and Conrad was still very much around and dangerous, a rogue grizzly battling for control of Montana. (He was still twenty years away from dying of alcoholism in Seattle, broke and supported by my upright father, whom he had not bothered to see once since the

251

ugly divorce when the boy was six years old. Why in Seattle? Had he been drummed out of his bailiwick, Montana? Whatever the reason, it died with my own father in 1954.)

Apparently when reporter Rush found he couldn't sell the article, he went to one of Conrad's prominent nephews at the Conrad National Bank in Great Falls, Montana, threatened blackmail, and was paid off with an undisclosed sum. The package somehow passed from the cousin to my father's personal papers, ultimately to end up in my mother's old trunk where I came upon it.

So there you have it—another suspect! Who is guilty—the Lady or the Tiger—or rather the Lady or the (I use the word advisedly) Grizzly? Furman favors the Lady. Macon (the more astute of the two lawyers) favors the Grizzly.

Is it possible that my own grandfather murdered my great-grandmother?

If he did, indeed, do it, think of the perfidy, the audacity and the enormity of the act by this hypocritical, latter-day Iago, this Reverend Dimsdale, this Preacher Davidson—to bring a man to trial for a crime that he himself had committed! The closet containing my family skeletons rattles over.

And to think that in addition to his name I have his genes in me. On my mother's side I am a direct descendant of Martha Custis Washington; of Robert Livingston; of admirals, lawyers, and statesmen; of the first American minister to Russia, a secretary of the navy, a secretary of state, and my kindly maternal grandfather, the first governor of Puerto Rico. Gentle and Yale-educated, all of them.

And on the other hand, there are the Conrads—rough, tough robber barons who were both feared and admired for their hardheaded independence and red-blooded vitality. Rebel cavalry guerillas during the Civil War; empire builders, grizzly hunters and manipulative politicians in Montana. And now possibly there's a murderer among them. Take the Barnaby blood—old J.B.'s taste for fine horses and women and his show business merchandising techniques; Josephine Barnaby's predilection for brandy and Adirondack guides; and my own staid Granny Mabel's adulterous affair with John Howard Conrad's business partners—and you have a pretty mixed group of genes to form a modern generation.

Were these genes responsible for such unorthodox behavior as my going into bullrings for glory, suffering serious gorings? For my headstrong brother's entering a Montana rodeo that caused him to lose his leg at the age of sixteen? For Conrad's other grandson, Barnaby Conrad Keeney, recklessly and singlehandedly wiping out a German machine gun nest in 1944 and winning the Silver Star? For Conrad's daughter Florence (who eloped to France with an American who was later shot while womanizing) winning the Croix de Guerre for bravery in World War I and rescuing the Louvre's Winged Victory of Samothrace from German hands in World War II? For my brother's children becoming a fishing guide in Montana and a salvage diver in Hawaii? And for my own children becoming artists and adventurers: one has a nightclub in Manhattan, one is a surfer-photographer last seen in Papeete hitching on a copra boat; while my eldest son writes and paints and likes to fish in the grizzly-infested streams of Alaska—without a guide, a .44 magnum strapped to his hip.

Where does it come from? Maybe genes don't have much bearing—nature versus nurture—on how families behave. A few of my cousins don't like to talk about the family "unpleasantness" to this day, but my youngest daughter thinks it's "kind of cool" that poor old Mrs. Barnaby, her great-great-grandmother, didn't just die in an old folks' home.

Barnaby—a name made famous by murder—dates back to the Plymouth Colony, where trial records show that an otherwise respectable James Barnaby was fined forty shillings for burning a parcel of pine knots belonging to Nathaniel Warren (of the *Mayflower* Warrens), an infraction not grave enough to keep James Barnaby from marrying one of the Warren granddaughters. For the next one hundred and fifty years the Barnabys were yeoman farmers and the name was unremarkable until the rise to prominence of the flamboyant and wealthy J. B. Barnaby—a man who wanted the name to last, but alas had no sons.

Today the name has virtually disappeared from New England, this helping to bury the memory of a wealthy widow who might or might not have been poisoned by her handsome doctor. Until the murder it had been a respected name in the East, and our family carried on that peculiar WASP American custom of converting a surname to a first name to preserve it from being lost in marriage. My father, myself, my eldest son, and my first cousin Barnaby Conrad Keeney (the late president of Brown University) were all saddled with the name that drew ridicule in grammar school and curiousity later ("Is it from Dickens' *Barnaby Rudge?*" we have all been asked *ad nauseam.)*

Nine decades have passed since the murder, and our family has been in California for four generations, a state where it is estimated that eighty percent of the current residents do not know the names of both their *grandparents.* Since the death of my father and cousin, I thought my son and I were the last of the legacy until my Rhode Island cousin Gloria Christensen, the granddaughter of J.B.'s brother Abner Barnaby, informed me that her own brother, her nephew, and another distant cousin all carry Barnaby as a first name.

I imagine these Eastern Barnabys as staid and proper—perhaps a false notion—just as they perhaps imagine us as suntanned, rootless hedonists—the Lost Tribes of Episcopalia wandering between the hills of San Francisco and the gardens of Montecito, where Granny Mabel escaped with "Pater" and my father after all the "revolting transactions" had finally left the Barnaby name, well, tainted.

So for what it is worth, all the evidence is in.

But then here is another surprise to add to this family scrapbook: Recently, out of the blue, I was sent several clippings dating from

1894 from the Denver Library that I had never seen before, despite my diligent research of the case.

"Graves did not kill himself!" screamed one of the newspaper's headlines. "A pine log was substituted for his body!" said another. "Bribery of the prison guards and funeral home admitted! Graves was hustled out of prison in a guard's uniform—rumored to be in Brazil with his wife and Mrs. Barnaby's money!"

I would like to think it was true—I hope so because I came to like Dr. Graves—but I doubt it.

"Who's to know?" as people with newspapers on their laps, rocking on porches all over the country, probably said about the inconclusive aftermath to this spellbinding American crime.

Indeed, who is to know?

DR. GRAVES NOT DEAD

It Is Said That His Suicide Was All a Fake.

A Pine Log Fills His Grave, and the Doctor Has Gone Abroad.

DENVER, Oct. 19.—The News publishes a sensational story to the effect that Dr. T. Thatcher Graves, the famous poisoner, who is supposed to have killed himself while in jail, is not dead. It is maintained a pine log occupied the coffin instead of his body.

The story is given on the authority of Charles N. Chandler, a wealthy citizen of Thompson Center, Conn., Graves' old home, and where the body is supposed to be buried.

Chandler and a fellow-townsman, Stephen Morse, are now here. They declare the coffin was opened at the grave against the protests of the widow and found to contain a pine log, and that the supposed dead doctor is now enjoying his freedom in a foreign country.

A rumor has been current here some time that the body carried from the County Jail was really wax and that the parties to the deception were some high officials of a secret organization. This rumor was strengthened by the refusal to allow the remains to be viewed except by the most intimate friends and by the further fact that the widow refused to allow the remains to be embalmed.

DEAD OR ALIVE.

Dr. Thatcher Graves, the Murderer, Is Said to Be Still Alive and That His Suicide Was Sham.

HIGH OFFICIALS IMPLICATED.

The readers of the DEMOCRAT will remember the sensational story of the murder of Mrs J. B. Barnaby, a wealthy widow lady, about  two years ago, the subsequent arrest of Dr. Thatcher Graves on a charge of murder, his trial and conviction at Denver and subsequent suicide. Thursday last the Denver News contained a startling story to the effect that the suicide was a sham, and that the doctor is now living, and it implicates prominent persons connected with a secret order. It says the supposed suicide in the local jail a few months ago was a trick whereby he secured his liberty.

It is maintained that a pine log occupied the coffin, instead of a body.

The story is given on the authority of Charles N. Chandler, a wealthy citizen of Thompson Center, Conn., Graves' old home, and where the body was supposed to be buried.